WHAT OT

Steve's desire to help those detached from the nurturing atmosphere of a loving church is powerfully expressed with a unique approach. By candidly addressing the primary issues that may have led to that detachment as well as the truth of God's intent for His people, he builds a soft but stable bridge welcoming them into the Father's open arms.

—*Dr. George O. Wood, General Superintendent of the Assemblies of God, Springfield, Missouri*

Steve Crino understands the unchurched person who often views Christianity cynically. He offers practical, relevant answers to common questions about the church. This book is a passionate plea from a deeply committed follower of Jesus to fellow believers to experience a true Spirit-empowered life.

—*Dr. Robert Spence, Chancellor of Evangel University, Springfield, Missouri*

Steven Crino loves people and is passionate about seeing them come into relationship with God through experiencing His power and presence in the local church. In the pages of this book, you will encounter Steve's passion as he reminds you of the church's true identity and world-changing mission!

—*John Lindell, Pastor of James River Church, Ozark, Missouri*

Steve Crino tells the whole truth and nothing but the truth about the church in this no-holds-barred book about his life inside and outside the church. If you've ever wondered why being part of a church is essential for followers of Christ, this book is for you!

—*Steve Pike, President, Urban Islands Project, Denver, Colorado*

A straightforward, honest, unvarnished look at the church. Steve's prayer is that each individual who reads this book experiences the genuine, unconditional love that Jesus offers. Since the local church is "God's design," Steve encourages each of us to find a local church that teaches God's Word and honors Jesus Christ. Jesus powerfully changed Steve's life, and He can do the same for every person who calls on the name of the Lord.

—*John M. Palmer, President,*
EMERGE Counseling Services, Akron, Ohio

I wholeheartedly agree with Steve Crino's statement, "The principles contained within this sacred book [the Bible] transcend time and culture and are still apropos today." His advice to find a Bible-believing, Bible-teaching church is of utmost importance. Not only should believers find a local church, but they should become involved in the church by supporting the church with tithes, with faithful attendance, and with ministry within the church.

—*Dr. Thomas E. Trask,*
former General Superintendent
of the Assemblies of God, Springfield, Missouri

Like a beautiful gem, the church has many facets. Most of us see only one or a few. In his long journey from drug user to senior pastor, Steve has had the privilege of viewing the church from many angles. In his book, *Church! Who Needs It?!* he invites us to walk with him and gain a perspective that will benefit us personally and enhance the church.

—*Owen C. Carr, veteran Assemblies of God minister,*
former college president, and author, Springfield, Missouri

Laugh. Cry. Be challenged. Learn. Steve's passion for you to grow comes through powerfully as he weaves scripture and many personal stories together in this easy-to-read and straightforward book. You will emerge with a whole new appreciation for how God can use His church to see you become all He intended.

—Brad Whipple, Pastor of
Seaport Community Church, Groton, Connecticut

C H U R C H !

WHO NEEDS IT?!

CHURCH!
WHO NEEDS IT?!

STEVE CRINO

TATE PUBLISHING
AND **ENTERPRISES**, LLC

Published by Tate Publishing & Enterprises, LLC
127 E. Trade Center Terrace | Mustang, Oklahoma 73064 USA
1.888.361.9473 | www.tatepublishing.com

Tate Publishing is committed to excellence in the publishing industry. The company reflects the philosophy established by the founders, based on Psalm 68:11,
"The Lord gave the word and great was the company of those who published it."

Book design copyright © 2015 by Tate Publishing, LLC. All rights reserved.
Cover design by Ivan Charlem Igot
Interior design by Honeylette Pino

Published in the United States of America

ISBN: 978-1-63449-935-4
1. Religion / General
2. Religion / Christian Life / Inspirational
15.05.11

To my beautiful and wonderful wife, Theresa,
and my three handsome sons Seth, Caleb, and Ezra

Besides God Himself, you are the
most important people in the entire world to me.
Each of you individually and all of us as a family mean
more to me than life itself. Of all the evidence in my life
displaying the goodness of God, you are the most pronounced.
You are the most wonderful fruit born from my decision
(by the grace of God) in 1981 to take "the road less traveled"
and follow Jesus Christ. Thank you for being you
and always loving and supporting me!
I love you more deeply and dearly
with each passing day. I could not
ask for a better family.
You are the best!

ACKNOWLEDGMENTS

I would like to express my gratitude to the following individuals and groups:

My late father, Rudolph Carmel Crino, you gave me life, trained me to fear the Lord, and cared for our family with undying devotion. Your honesty, character, strength, and integrity were shaping me when I was too young and inexperienced to realize it. I regret that you are no longer around for me to tell you how much I have come to appreciate who you were.

My mother, Felecina Crino, your prayers for me during my prodigal years were the avenues of God's grace that kept me from death many times and stopped the tide of natural consequences that would have damaged my life indelibly. Your sincerity, dedication, kindness, love, and tender heart model the character of the Savior wonderfully. We have walked through many difficulties together, and your integrity has never wavered through any of them.

My spiritual mother, Catherine Deion, the love you showed for me and the joy you displayed were the things I had not noticed in any other "religious" person. Your boldness to tell me the gospel of grace was essential to my salvation. I would not have listened to someone with a soft-sell approach at that time. I was too halfhearted and thickheaded. Thank you for the patience you displayed in answering the questions of my hungry heart. You were the primary vessel who led me to Christ, Who turned my entire life around! I would be dead or in jail if not for you!

Wayne Deion, you were so much like me that I could relate to you yet so incredibly different that I wanted what you had. Most godly people I had known seemed to lack masculinity and were odd (even spooky). You were a physically fit "regular" guy who simply loved the Lord and had a true life-changing encounter with Him. In Psalm 142:4, King David wrote, "No one cares for my soul." I could never claim such a thing because of you and your mom. Thank you!

Professor Sharon Rooney, though I was thirty-six years old and had been in ministry for over a decade when I became your student, you recognized a talent in me no one else had. Your gracious words to me when I would submit writings to you touched me deeper than I have ever fully explained to you. Please know that this book was written because of your comments and encouragement. Thank you from the bottom of my heart!

Owen Carr, my good friend and mentor. When I asked you to be my mentor, I will never forget how quickly nor how kindly you responded. I had no idea the depth of friendship that would come from those monthly conversations together. Besides always being supportive and the person who most reflects the character of Jesus I have ever known, you took the time to review my book and gave me sound advice. Thank you for taking me under your wing in so many ways.

Rebecca Gullion, though you had never worked closely with a northeast "eye-talian" with a type-A personality, you graciously and faithfully served under my leadership with amazing excellence. As our children's pastor, you also had a deep impact on the life of my two oldest sons. Further, you reviewed my book and gave me *incredibly* detailed sound guidance. I cannot imagine how many hours you put in to do that, but your insights and advice were priceless. You are an amazing woman of God, and I have the highest respect for you. Thank you!

Dick Hardy, you have far more experience in writing and publications than I do. Thank you for taking the time to guide and direct me. Your counsel and encouragement were key to the completion and success of this project.

Group of Quiet Supporters, my book was completed, but I was unable financially to publish it. The church we started was unable to pay me any salary for an entire year building up to the final preparations of this manuscript. I simply sent an e-mail to friends across the country explaining my situation. I offered to give a complimentary copy of this book to anyone who would donate $25 or more to its publication. I was pleasantly surprised at their kind generosity, and it was yet another divine confirmation of the necessity of this book's publication. Your encouragement was the final *blast* of momentum I needed to proceed. Thank you so much! You know who you are.

CONTENTS

PREFACE

Wow! You may have noticed that you're already on page 52, and you just started! How cool is that? There is nothing wrong with the page numbering, and you do not need to return your copy of the book. This is intentional. Why?

I know when I first start a book, it seems a bit overwhelming, like the first step of a journey. A friend may call just then and ask, "Hey, what's up?"

To which I would reply, "I just started a book...I'm on page 2...long way to go."

But with this book starting at page 52, if you have a friend who calls to ask you a similar question, you can say, "Hey, just started a book, and I'm already on page 52! Wow! It's just flowing!" You feel better about it, your friend is impressed, and as an author, I'm happy because *you* are happy. Everyone wins!

So read on, my friend, it's already flowing![1]

* * *

Many Americans do not really seem to have much of a problem with God per se, but they do with His professed followers. Many of us—oh, who am I kidding—*all* of us have probably had some kind of negative encounter with people who profess to be religious or spiritual, yet their attitudes and actions do not support the claim.

I grew up in Rhode Island and was raised in the Roman Catholic Church. My parents were two of the most devout and sincere churchgoers one would ever find. They truly gave it their best efforts to live what they believed. Throughout my childhood, I attended church with them, and the only time I recall my parents missing church was when my father was dying.

Like everyone who attempts to be spiritual, they weren't perfect, but they were definitely sincere. Descendants of Italian immigrants, they were first-generation Americans who grew up during the Depression. They were hard workers with a high moral code. In fact, I never heard them lie or saw them intentionally harm another human being my entire life. I remember trying to get my mother to say I was not home in my teen years when another young person called me who I really did not want to talk to. She flatly refused! At that time, I did not like it, but now I could not even express how much I appreciate what my parents contributed to my spiritual journey.

Despite all that, I saw what seemed to me as phoniness and hypocrisy in the church, and it really turned me off even at a young age. I remember seeing people participating in the religious services, and then, as soon as we got in the parking lot to leave, they were swearing at each other, making obscene gestures out the window and acting no different (*maybe even worse!*) than the people who did not attend church! Even as a child, something about that just did not seem right.

When I hit the ripe old age of fourteen, you know, that age where you're certain you know everything and older people have no clue about *real* life, the church just did not seem to have anything to do with reality. I was a kid with my hormones in high gear, bored out of my socks with life, and just trying to figure out what it even meant to be a man. I was being offered drugs, booze, and pornography at every turn. It seemed to me that the main message of the traditional church, as sincere as they were, was simply *be good*. While that is certainly a great (though nebulous) goal, they did not offer any compelling reasons to simply deny my pleasures because some supreme being said so. Also, they certainly provided no power to be successful at it, whether the reasons were motivating or not. As one author put it, "Telling people that what they are doing is wrong does not give them the power to stop doing it."[2] How true, and yet that was my experience.

To add to that, my encounters with professing religious people continued to be mostly negative. I remember walking into church and a somewhat elderly usher dressed in a suit stood over a table where we were to put money as we walked in. Frankly, he looked like he had been baptized in vinegar, had not smiled in about a decade, and I got the distinct impression he was looking down his nose at me every time I came.

So the love and help a troubled teenager like me could have received while I was still at least somewhat open to it just did not seem available. On top of that, the way the adults looked and acted toward me seemed judgmental and critical. I did not feel very wanted. My unasked question was, "If the god we worship is so loving, why aren't His people?" Maybe you can relate.

At that age, I really did not look or act the stereotypical part of a religious person. That's for sure. I fit the stereotype of a teenager in the 1970s. I had long hair; was rebellious against authority; listened to the music of Black Sabbath, KISS, and Alice Cooper; wore a jean jacket that advertised marijuana (my poor, innocent parents did not have a clue); smoked; and had a really foul mouth. Some parents did not even want their kids to hang around me and, looking back now, who could blame them? Yet in the midst of that, no one asked nor did they seem to care *why* I was that way. Again, the only message I grasped was *be good*. It seemed to me that God was love as long as I was good; otherwise, He stood with His almighty arms crossed, looking down at me with a frown of disgust, pointing His holy finger at me, and waiting to judge me. With this mental image of God, it really is not too difficult to see why I did not want anything to do with church. I do not recall making a conscious decision, but somehow, in all my teenage wisdom, I simply felt, "Church! Who needs it?"

It was not that I did not believe in God's existence; I just did not understand what He was like or how to really have a relationship with Him. Also I could not understand the reason behind all the rules and definitely had no power within me to keep them. Did God really care about me? I figured He did, but there was some kind of disconnect between Him and me. This is how many people feel today. If you can relate to this and feel as I did, I believe this book is for you!

I do not profess to know all the answers. In fact, I am not sure I even know all the questions, but the scope of this book is simply to answer the underlying question, "Church! Who needs it?" If you're searching for answers and seeking truth, I hope this book will be helpful to you. The good news is there is a supreme being who sincerely cares about you and is deeply committed to bringing you closer to Him. I pray he uses these chapters to show you *what a priceless treasure you are to Him!*

Steve Crino

1

THE CORE

WHAT GOD DO YOU SEEK?

We live in a world with many supposed gods. A god is something or someone that we look to for strength, guidance, and help to live life. A god is what or who we look to as superior to us whom we worship and draw strength from. It seems obvious that we have an innate desire to worship something beyond ourselves. Some worship money. Some worship their profession or climbing the corporate ladder. Others worship another person like a lover. Candidly speaking, there are too many things to list. We Americans often look down on what we consider primitive peoples as we see their faces on the television while they worship a totem pole or express some seemingly outdated kind of worship.

Yet the truth is that, when people draw their strength from things, pursuits, people, or the multitude of other gods, they are just as guilty of unsophisticated idolatry as those they look down on. My point in saying all that is, when we use the word *god*, that can mean almost anything or anyone. In such a diverse society, it could mean Buddha, Allah, Jesus Christ, or a number of other Eastern gurus. It could mean too many things to consider in the scope of this book.

Some years ago, while I was working in a machine shop, I was explaining to a friend how Jesus Christ had dramatically changed my life for the better. This naturally led to questions from both of us. He wanted to try to understand how that happened. I was curious to know how he felt about Jesus. I will never forget his answer. He said he thought that Jesus was an alien from another planet! My curiosity peaked, and so I asked him to explain. He said that Jesus was dropped off here by terrestrial beings as an experiment. When I asked him why he thought Jesus died then, he replied that the experiment apparently failed. That was one I had not heard before!

Another time, while I was a student in a trade school, I got into a discussion with one of my professors about Christianity. He said that everyone who is not an atheist is a Christian. His logic seemed so faulty that I queried him further by asking him if he then meant that Buddhists are Christians, and his answer was affirmative!

To add to the struggle, when Americans use the word *church*, we can mean a number of things. Our family's religious heritage, our denomination, the building we worship at, etc. When someone says they are a churchgoer, do they mean Baptist? Catholic? Protestant? If it's Baptist, which *strand* of Baptist? Southern Baptist? American Baptist? Independent Baptist? If it's Catholic, is it Roman Catholic, United Catholic, Greek Orthodox, or Charismatic? If it's Protestant, is it Lutheran? Methodist, Presbyterian? Seventh-Day Adventist or one of the other two hundred denominations that fall under the heading of Protestantism? Obviously, it can be very confusing! In light of all that, let me explain what the scope of this book will be.

First of all, the fact that you are reading this book implies that you have a desire for spirituality or are on a quest for truth. According to religious research guru George Barna, 4 to 8 percent of Americans do not believe in God or identify themselves as atheist or agnostic.[3] You may be part of that crowd. However, with such a variety of what people may mean when they use the word *god*, the thrust of this book needs to be clear. This book is written to help people with a belief in the God of the Bible (or at least an *openness* to it). He is revealed in the Hebrew scriptures (also called the Old Testament) and His purposes for humanity are fulfilled in the Christian scriptures (referred to as the New Testament). If that overall system of belief does not describe you to some degree, this book may be of little help to you.

Those who do believe in (and by that I mean *trust in, cling to and rely on*) the God of the Bible take those writings as the basis of all that they believe. It is the very foundation that supports the rest of the building. The Bible gives the necessary instructions and principles to make quality decisions for every situation in life.

Frankly, the word *believe* has come to mean little in our fast-paced technological world. For many, it simply means they agree with the facts they are aware of as long as it allows them to maintain control of their decisions and their preferred level of comfort. *Believe* is typically a word of intellectual assent, which has little, if any, connection to one's behavior, conduct, or lifestyle.

However, when it comes to belief in the God of the Bible, the word *believe* carries with it the idea of obedience or adherence to its instructions, commandments, and principles. To truly believe what God says or instructs in His Word certainly demands actually ordering one's attitude and actions to agree with it. If not, in what sense is there any genuine measurable belief? As I once heard a singer say on stage, "One only truly believes that which motivates them to action."[4] I encourage you to look at that last sentence a few times before reading on and really consider it. Readers who believe (or again, at least have an open mind to believe) in the Bible as God's message to humanity are who this book is written for. If the god that you seek is the God of the Bible, read on, my friend.

2

THE CONFUSION

WHAT THE CHURCH IS NOT

Sometimes considering first what something is *not* helps to determine what it is. As you can see already, discovering truth is not for wimps or the halfhearted. Perhaps you are one who has had experience in the church world. While there was a time that that could be assumed in the United States, that time has passed. We have many people from many different cultures, countries, and backgrounds in our society today. When we add to that the fact that many turned their back on the traditional church during the revolutions (sexual, authority, etc.) of the 1960s and we have reaped decades of the result of that, it is no wonder that many in our country have no clue what the church is or is not. I can tell you this: it is not what most assume it to be. Let me explain.

There is a well-known bumper sticker which proclaims, Christians Aren't Perfect, Just Forgiven. While that is a true statement, I have never liked that saying. Frankly, it seems like a cop out. Is it just an excuse for behavior that does not reconcile with a profession to follow someone as "perfect" as Jesus Christ? Or does it simply assert the idea, "Do not evaluate Christ by my imperfect behavior?" If it is the former, it appears to be little more than a poor justification for not practicing what one professes. However, if it is the latter, the concept is to direct one's focus onto Jesus instead of his imperfect followers. That is what human beings really need to do, and yet, many struggle with that. Of course, it is a reasonable expectation to look for some Christ-like behavior and attitudes in those who profess to follow Him. However, the church is not made of people who are *identical* to Jesus, just those sincerely *trying* to be.

Even though most would deny it, a major problem in people's estimation of the local church is that many visit religious services or evaluate those professing to be spiritual, expecting perfect people. Of course, they do not find such people because none exist! Most would agree with the statement, "There is no perfect church." Frankly, if there was, it would no longer be once I entered it because I am galaxies away from being perfect and but a poor reflection (at best) of the man called Jesus. If you do not believe me, ask my wife and kids!

Another problem is with the people who regularly attend. Feeling the pressure to be flawless while realizing their own imperfections yet wrestling with their human pride, they simply struggle to admit their failings. After all, no one wants to be labeled a *hypocrite*. As religious people come to realize their need to live a moral and holy life, including the desire to spread the word about God's love, they feel inadequate as a sound representative thereof.

I believe, and my experience has confirmed, that nonchurch-goers have little aversion to God or to Jesus Christ, but they do with His professing followers. One complaint is that they claim to be holy but have obvious imperfections that they will not admit. Basically, they come across as holier-than-thou when it is obvious that they usually struggle with the same issues and failures as those who make no such spiritual claims. I believe this is a legitimate grievance.

It has been said that "the church is a hospital for sinners," and such it must be. Those who want to live a godly life are not perfect in every attitude and action and should avoid *pretending* that they are. Pretending to be keeps people from receiving the help or strength they need to overcome their own issues. Phoniness keeps people trapped in their painful patterns. Honest admission of struggle combined with openness to change puts struggling people on the right path to true help. Followers of Jesus are fellow strugglers on the same journey sincerely trying to honor the God we love. No matter what title, office, or status one has, we are all made of the same stuff. While our struggles may sound and look a little different, the heart of them is not.

The consumer mentality of our time and culture is another major contributor to the weak impact of most churches in our society. Further, it is indicative of our fast-paced, impatient, and self-centered ways. Many people treat the local church like a local Walmart or Target. They have come to get what they want and, if they do not find it at one store, they simply go to the next—no big deal. Loyalty seems to be a thing of the past, and heaven help any church leader who suggests such a thing. Images of Jim Jones or David Koresh flash through the minds of congregants when they hear the suggestion. *Loyalty? Is he kidding? I can go wherever I want!*

Many attend local churches with little thought of how they can contribute to that church's mission or what they can *give*. Most come to see what they can *get* out of it. While being in a local church that provides certain things to assist people and their families in developing into mature disciples is important, why are so few willing to pay the price to help the church provide such things? Like loyalty, precious few want to hear about the sacrifice and hard work needed to have a healthy church.

Is it really such a curious thing that people often treat religious services like going to a movie when most churches are set up like a theater? Think about it. There is typically a raised stage or platform where the performers play their parts so to speak. The attendees watch the *performance*, if you will, and respond emotionally as seems appropriate. Afterward, most go home, grab a bite to eat, and talk about the performance they just saw while making little change in their personal life. Besides the spiritual dimension of a typical church service (e.g., songs of worship, preaching, prayer, etc.), how different is that from taking in the latest flick? The theater does not expect much from the patrons except that they pay their way and support their products. Sadly, the call to follow Jesus from most churches in our culture today expects little more from their attendees. Further, if most who come had any expectations put on them, many would just switch stores…uh…I mean theaters…no, no…I mean *churches*. (You get the point!)

The church is not a country club for saints. Though it is a place to come and receive, it is far more than that! It is more than a place to evaluate all the player's performances. We are not to stand back like Ebert and Roeper and criticize the church worker's "performance."

Now I know as you are reading this, you are probably thinking of the many imperfections in your own life and in those you have known who professed to be followers of Jesus. Though we will look at more of that in chapter 4, suffice to say for now, no human representation in such a fallen, imperfect, and sinful world could ever adequately characterize such a holy, perfect, and sinless being like God.

3

THE CLARITY

WHAT THE CHURCH IS

As was mentioned in the first chapter, people in our culture mean many things when they use the word *church*. However, most of us think of some branch of the Christian faith. Though we use it as such, the word never refers to a building in the New Testament. It refers to sinners who have repented of their sins and placed personal faith in the Lord Jesus Christ as their only means of salvation and have thus been born again as the savior described in the third chapter of the gospel of John.

This is the original *Nick by Nite* story! A religious leader named Nicodemus came to Jesus undercover of night to ask him some questions. He was part of what was in essence the Jewish supreme court of his day known as the Sanhedrin. It was made up of approximately seventy learned elders who knew the scriptures quite well. The problem was that this group had rejected Jesus as the Christ.

Jesus' fame was spreading everywhere. News of Him healing the lame, the blind, the deaf, casting out demons, and even raising the dead was impossible to keep contained. His effectiveness at explaining God and meeting people's deepest need so surpassed that of these religious men that it enraged them with jealousy. However, by the time of Jesus' conversation with Nicodemus in John chapter 3, this moral, well-respected elder had come to realize that Jesus was not just some crazed or cultic religious figure. He said to Jesus, "Rabbi, we know You are a teacher who has come from God. For no one could perform the miraculous signs You are doing if God were not with Him."[5]

Jesus basically ignored his comment but moved to the deeper issue of Nicodemus's heart—his quest for real spiritual truth. He said, "I tell you the truth, no one can see the kingdom of God unless he is born again."[6] Since humanity's fall from grace in the Garden of Eden,[7] every person is born in the *conditions* that resulted from our first parents' sin. However, each one of us enter into the *guilt* of their *original sin* as we understand God's standard and willfully defy it like Adam and Eve did.[8] Since sin brings death[9] or separation from God, each person's spirit is dead, in terms of the ability to connect with our Creator. As a dead body can no longer respond to the stimuli of this world, neither can we respond appropriately to God once we have sinned as the first sinners did.

The physical union of our earthly parents brought about a physical birth. However, since our spirit is dead in sin,[10] and nothing unholy will ever enter heaven,[11] for a human to be suitable for that holy place requires some kind of transformation and removal of that sinful condition. That is where being born again comes in. In that conversation with Nicodemus in John chapter 3, Jesus went on to reiterate the need for this spiritual rebirth two more times in verses 5–7.

> Jesus answered, "I tell you the truth, no one can *enter* the kingdom of God unless he is born of water and the Spirit. Flesh gives birth to flesh, [i.e., a physical union leads to a physical birth] but the Spirit gives birth to spirit. [i.e., a spiritual union lead by the Holy Spirit brings about a spiritual birth] You should not be surprised at My saying, "You[12] *must* be born again." (emphasis added)

It is critical to note that in verse 3, Jesus used the word *see*, and in verse 5, he used the word *enter*. Therefore, until one has experienced this spiritual birth, they cannot *see* (i.e., perceive or understand) the spiritual truths of God's kingdom, and they can *enter* neither those realities nor the actual place of that existence (i.e., heaven and/or the New Jerusalem). In 1 Corinthians 2:14, Paul the Apostle confirms this inability of one who has not been born again to grasp God's truths. He writes, "The man without the Spirit does not accept the things that come from the Spirit of God, for they are foolishness[13] to him, and he *cannot* [emphasis added] understand them, because they are spiritually discerned."

Plainly, this experience is essential to anyone who wants to understand the God of the Bible and enter His kingdom. In fact, according to Jesus, there is no other way for that to happen. Being born again is not a new religious fad. Whether a person or religious entity uses the *phrase* or *title* to define themselves as such or not, the *experience* is indispensable. One's level of education, influence, status, or morality has no more to do with spiritual birth than their physical birth. A union brings birth in both realms. One can no more call God their father in the truest sense than one could call a man who is not their physical father by that title.[14] Though conception begins the life between father and child, the birth starts the living out of it.

CHURCH! WHO NEEDS IT?!

The reason I share all that is to be clear who is and is not part of what is called the universal church versus the local church according to the Bible. Not everyone who attends religious services at a church building is actually part of the universal church, but all those who have been born again are. That is critical to understand.

The word *church* and its derivatives, is used 114 times in the New International Version of the Bible.[15] The original Greek word *ekklesia* refers to "gatherings of people in some kind of assembly...the New Testament understands 'church' to refer to the visible expression of the gathered followers of Jesus Christ who have been grafted into a community created by God."[16] So much is implied in this definition. Being a *follower* of Christ certainly implies mimicking or being like him in some way. Sounds lofty in describing the church, doesn't it? That is not how I perceived what I witnessed in the church when I was a boy. If the people I encountered were a fair representation of Jesus Christ, nothing would have ever attracted me to Him. But you see that is exactly the point.

I know it is not my place to judge who is and is not a true follower, but clearly, the spirit of the vast majority of people in the "churches" I encountered did not seem to bear much (*if any*) resemblance to the man called Jesus Christ as He is described in the Bible. Would Jesus put on a religious show while in church but then be rude or obscene in the parking lot once the religious service was over? Surely not! We will further consider the issue of hypocrisy in chapter 4.

When a person decides to turn away from a lifestyle of sin with God's help and puts their personal faith in the Lord Jesus Christ,[17] their spirit is born, and since they were already born once (physically), the savior called it being born *again*. These are the people that make up the universal church. Though those who are genuinely part of the bride of Christ (the church) are not perfect in their daily practical lives, they do not *continue* to live a *lifestyle* that embraces sin as a consistent pattern or tone of their lives; indeed, they *cannot*.[18] A new and holy nature is part of that spiritual birth, and so, even though the individual will struggle with the patterns of their sinful nature, the desire to sin diminishes the more they feed their spirit with God's Word. Further, a new power from the Holy Spirit empowers them to live a life of purity. As stated earlier, understanding the new birth is critical in this entire matter.

In fact, it is no exaggeration to say that the entire New Testament is about the rebirth that brings salvation and changes the heart from a heart of stone to one that is soft and pliable in God's hands. Further, the new birth is prophesied about throughout the Old Testament.

Centuries before the man Jesus was born, God spoke through the prophet Ezekiel in chapter 36:25–27 of the book by his name. He said,

> I will sprinkle clean water on you, and you will be clean; I will cleanse you from all your impurities and from all your idols. I will give you a new heart and *put a new spirit in you*; I will remove from you your heart of stone and give you a heart of flesh [emphasis added]. And I will put my Spirit in you and move you to follow My decrees and be careful to keep My laws. (emphasis added)

This speaks of the new birth Jesus teaches about in John chapter 3. People may be able to change their *habits*, but only God Himself can change the *heart*. In that spiritual birth, one's heart is turned from being hard toward God to being soft and pliable to His touch. Their spirit that was dead in sin[19] is raised to life by God's Spirit. Then, and *only* then, His laws or ways are no longer viewed as outsiders trying to get into the person's thinking, but they become part of the individual's new spiritual DNA.

The prophet Jeremiah agrees as his book records in chapter 31:31–34,

"The time is coming," declares the LORD, "when I will make a new covenant with the house of Israel and with the house of Judah. It will not be like the covenant I made with their forefathers when I took them by the hand to lead them out of Egypt, because they broke My covenant, though I was a husband to them," declares the LORD. "This is the covenant I will make with the house of Israel after that time," declares the LORD. "I will put My law *in their minds* and write it *on their hearts.* [emphasis added] I will be their God, and they will be My people. No longer will a man teach his neighbor, or a man his brother, saying, 'Know the LORD,' because *they will all know Me,* from the least of them to the greatest," declares the LORD. "For I will forgive their wickedness and will remember their sins no more."

The forefathers broke the covenant[20] with God because they still were dead in their sins and did not have the Spirit of God within them yet. They were literally *incapable* of keeping God's laws, having no power from *within,* only *exterior* rules. As it was then, so it is now. Only those who have had this spiritual rebirth (which only God can cause[21]) have the inner impetus to walk in God's ways. It is at that point, and *only* at that point, that His ways are with*in,* no longer with*out.*

If you are like me and so many others, I thought I was a Christian before I had that rebirth. However, I lived a lifestyle of sin and had little tolerance for holy things. I was no more a child of God and could in no legitimate way call him my Father, yet I deceived myself into thinking He was. This is the state of many who attend religious services and more than likely the state of many I encountered in my early years shaping my view of people alleging (or in their defense, *attempting*) to be spiritual. It would seem wise to keep that in mind as we consider our impressions of churchgoers and hopefully move beyond human failure to discover genuine truth.

The church is an interdependent group of born-again believers *in* and obedient followers *of* the Lord Jesus Christ as He is represented in the orthodox New Testament.

No matter what denominational name they bear or where they choose to worship, provided the teachings of the Bible are the foundation and focus, these people are *the church*. It is not about showing up at a building so many times a week or going through particular routines and rituals as much as it is about being truly devoted to the person of God and what He puts forth in the Bible. You may have heard this before, but going to church makes you no more a Christian than going to McDonald's makes you a hamburger or sitting in a garage makes you a car. The heart of the matter is always the matter of the heart.

The church, also called the body of Christ in the New Testament, is the physical representation of God on earth. Yes, it is a very flawed one, but God has designed it to be His beacon to this world. A local church's effectiveness or lack thereof in being that beacon in practical ways *does not change that that is His plan.*

In what is called the Sermon on the Mount beginning in the fifth chapter of Matthew's gospel, Jesus called His followers (all of them, not just the clergy) to be "the salt of the earth." As salt *preserves*, so a righteous lifestyle of God's people is to preserve society from slipping deeper into moral decay. As salt makes one *thirsty*, so the life and passion of believers is to create a *thirst* for God in others. As salt *seasons* food to make it more enjoyable, so Christ's followers should make life more enjoyable for their community, emulating the love and character of Jesus to those they come in contact with.

In that same public speech, Jesus called His followers to be the "light of the world." In the New Testament, light often represents truth, as well as godly living and purity, while darkness often represents falsehood, sin, and evil. As light scatters darkness, so should the life of believers scatter the darkness of sin and evil around them. As light makes the right and best path clearer, so should the lives and counsel of professing Christians make the right and best paths of life plain—the decisions that would please and honor God.

The church is called the body of Christ for several reasons. One of which is that since Jesus (who is the head, i.e., leader and source[22]) returned to heaven, He has left His people to represent Him to this world (i.e., to *be* Him). He gave His people a mission, which is spelled out in all four Gospels and in the book of Acts.[23] Basically, the mission is to tell the glorious good news of God's love demonstrated to the whole world by giving His only Son to take our punishment on the cross. By raising Him from the dead three days later, the Father then affirmed that all Jesus had said and done was legit. This was to verify that He had retained salvation for all His followers. He also gave us His authority to advance His kingdom in this dark world.

Not only is the church referred to as a *body* in the New Testament, it is also spoken of as a *bride* (or the bride of Christ). This speaks of a loving partnership. It creates a mental picture of an unbreakable union with similar goals, desires, and direction. One of Jesus followers named Paul said the union of husband and wife is an illustration of the connection between Christ and His people. He was instructing the local church in the city of Ephesus about family matters including the beautiful union of marriage. In doing so, he quoted God's original intent for a couple in Ephesians 5:31–32 where he wrote,

> For this reason a man will leave his father and mother and be united to his wife, and the two will become one flesh. This is a profound mystery—*but I am talking about Christ and the church* [emphasis added].

To the local church in the city of Corinth, he also wrote, "He who unites himself with the Lord is one with Him in spirit."[24] As a bride commits herself to her groom and the two are united becoming one in purpose, goals, and direction so those who commit themselves to the Lord Jesus Christ become one with Him. In a very real sense, it is holy matrimony.

As the loving couple forsakes all other lovers, the heavenly Groom and all united to Him forsake all others and become united, married, if you will. Like a sincere husband protects, defends, and cares for his bride, so the Lord Jesus Christ does those things for His followers.

Lastly, Jesus' followers are not only called a *body* and a *bride*, the New Testament also refers to them as a *building*. As every brick, board, nail, and wire all come together to be a beautiful edifice representing what was in the mind of the architect, so followers of Christ are united to represent the One who designed her. The great architect Himself![25]

Though many lessons could be drawn from these three biblical illustrations, one thing to point out is that they all speak of *interdependency*. In other words, each part depends on the others to come together and operate within their designed function for one overall, unified purpose.

God designed the local church to be a place filled with love, compassion, and His genuine, life-changing power. *Therein is the problem.* The vast majority of Americans have not discovered church to be those things *at all*. In fact, many have found it to be the exact opposite and experienced more camaraderie and connection among those who profess no belief (or a *minimal* one at best) in the God of the Bible!

4

THE QUANDARY

THE PROBLEMS IN THE CHURCH

May I warn you before you read this chapter? This section is raw. It is an honest and candid look at the problems in the church, which are often glossed over in the name of optimism. While I am all for being positive, it should never be at the expense of the truth. Chapter 5 is somewhat of a rebuttal to all the problems discussed here in chapter 4. If you are a religious person entrenched in traditional views of the church, this chapter may really irritate you. However, please consider, problems can never be corrected until reality is faced. This chapter is a reality check.

Still dare to read on? Okay, you have been warned. Strap on your seat belt and get ready for a rocky ride!

The book of Acts records what life was like in the early days of the church. It is filled with amazing accounts of God breaking into this world and wonderfully interrupting the normal flow of humanity. In the New Testament, this began during the life of Jesus of course. That is why Luke, the writer of the book of Acts begins his writing to a Jewish leader in this way:

> In my former book, Theophilus, I wrote about all that Jesus *began* to do and to teach until the day he was taken up to heaven, after giving instructions through the Holy Spirit *to the apostles he had chosen.*" [emphasis added]

The clear implication is that what Jesus began would then continue through his apostles. In fact, so much occurred through these twelve men that many have suggested that Acts be renamed the Acts of the Apostles. Because these amazing events were supernatural and clearly a God-thing; however, others suggest it be named the Acts of the Holy Spirit. I would like to suggest it should be named the Acts of the Holy Spirit through the Apostles. Okay, enough of the name game! The point is that what is recorded in the book of Acts are supernatural phenomenon, a record of God invading humanity and turning things right side up!

With that in mind, can we simply be candid? When we look at the New Testament and understand what God intended Christians and the church to be, and then we look at her condition here in the good ole' U-S of A, they do not coincide. In fact, there seems to be an uncrossable chasm between the two. The only way to *not* notice the vast gulf between what occurred in the New Testament and what the church in America is like today is to either ignore or suppress the obvious. Followers of Jesus proclaim that God has immense supernatural insight and ability. Yet compared to our lives and our impact on the world around us, the two simply do not reconcile! This ain't rocket science, friend!

When an honest and sincere comparison is made between the church today in America and the New Testament, the question arises, "What happened?"

John Wesley, one of the founders of the Methodist church said, "The world would be Christian were it not for *Christians*."[26]

Let's consider ten issues in the present church in America that clearly contradict the New Testament's display of the early church. However, before we do, let me clarify a couple of things. First of all, it is clear from the New Testament that the church is God's idea, not man's. The church is the bride of Christ, and any true follower of Jesus will love her like He does, despite of all her flaws.[27] The claim to have a good relationship with Jesus (the bridegroom) and yet avoid, neglect, or dislike His bride makes as much sense as someone expecting to have a good relationship with me yet having a disdain for my wife. I want to be clear that while taking a truly honest assessment of the church is critical, responding to those issues while avoiding the affirmation and support of the Lord's bride is unscriptural.

Secondly, there are also a multitude of positive things about the local church, and all of these issues are true of every congregation. That being stated, they do need to be considered with an honest and candid heart. This writer sincerely hopes and prays that every reader will prayerfully consider them with such a tone.

WHAT'S LOVE GOT TO DO WITH IT? (LOVELESSNESS)

I am not much of a fan of MTV, but when I ministered to teenagers, I felt a real need to keep up with it to know what was going on in their world. In 1984, Tina Turner released her famous album *Private Dancer*. The song on that album that was mostly responsible for its success was entitled, "What's Love Got To Do With It?" It was arguably the most successful song of her decades-long career and was eventually the title of a movie about her, which debuted in 1993.[28] I can still remember seeing her strutting up to a young couple with her typical rebellious demeanor as she sang out, "What's love got to do with it? What's love but a secondhand emotion?" Sadly, that's how many feel about attendance at or involvement in the local church. In fact, that's how many feel about religion in general and professing Christians in particular.

Probably one of the best known statements in the New Testament was written by one of Jesus' closest friends, the apostle John. The verse says, "God is love."[29] It is important to point out that it does not say, God *provides* love, or God *inspires* love. It says plainly God is love. Love is the very nature and essence of the person of God. Love is not simply one of His emotions or characteristics. It is not just something He brings about; it is who He is. That is exactly where the rub is.

In the thirteenth chapter of John's gospel, there is an account of Jesus demonstrating to His closest friends what was to be the distinguishing mark of His followers—love. It was shortly before Jesus' arrest when He was gathered with the twelve, His closest friends, to give them some final instructions before the plot against Him would culminate at the cross.

As they gathered in that intimate setting for the Last Supper, their feet were very dirty from the dusty streets of the Middle East. It is important to point out that these were not paved streets where primarily the friction of rubber tires passed over them. These were not kept clean by a sweeper or lined by nicely manicured shrubbery and freshly-mowed, weed-free green grass. No way! Because of the heavy-footed traffic of both man and beasts (and whatever they left behind), walking on these roadways would leave one's feet—to borrow the modern term—gross!

With all that as a backdrop, consider the custom of that time and culture as we reflect on the account in John 13. When guests entered a home or dwelling, it was customary for slaves to wash their dirty, disgusting feet. As the twelve chatted together with Jesus that night before this meal, they all knew full well that someone had to wash their feet. For some unknown reason, it appears that the usual household slave was not present for the task. Imagine the tension and conviction as they watched Jesus, their master, suddenly take a towel and basin to begin doing the job of a slave! Of all people! Certainly silence filled the air because each one realized that their pride and desire for importance, power, and position stood in the way of them doing what should have been done by *them*, not Jesus. No wonder Simon Peter protested at first! He said, "No, you shall never wash my feet."[30] When Jesus explained it was necessary, Peter enthusiastically complied.

John goes on to further say,

> When he had finished washing their feet, he put on His clothes and returned to His place. "Do you understand what I have done for you?" he asked them. "You call Me 'Teacher' and 'Lord,' and rightly so, for that is what I am. Now that I, your Lord and Teacher, have washed your feet, you also should wash one another's feet. I have set you an example that you should do as I have done for you. I tell you the truth, no servant is greater than his master, nor is a messenger greater than the one who sent him. Now that you know these things, you will be blessed if you do them.

He set the stage for them to show their love for each other by serving one another, even if it meant taking the lowest duty like a slave.

Jesus' entire ministry was different than any other professing prophet or religious figure who preceded Him. Hence, there was to be something different about those who would follow (i.e., imitate) Him as well. He went on to say,

> "A new command I give you: Love one another. As I have loved you, so you must love one another. *By this all men will know that you are My disciples, if you love one another.*" (emphasis added)

It is not that loving others was "a new command" per se; it was recorded in the Old Testament *long* before Jesus was born. Every Jewish child grew up learning that command and knew it quite well. In Leviticus 19:18, centuries before that first Christmas, God commanded His people to "love your neighbor as yourself." Jesus quoted this verse in Matthew 22 as the second greatest command in the entire Bible, closely following the command to love God with all our being.

Jesus' command in John 13 was about love being, not just an element in the day-to-day lives of His followers, nor even a *major* one. No, as love is the very nature and essence of God, so it is to be the very essence and nature of His people—the church. You may want to go back and read that last line again. Loving one's neighbor was not new in the sense that it was never commanded before. Rather, it was "new" in terms of being the distinguishing mark, the most pronounced characteristic of this new spiritual sect eventually called *Christians*.[31] In 1 John 3:16 (the *other* John 3:16), John the Apostle wrote, "This is how we know what love is: Jesus Christ laid down his life for us. *And we ought to lay down our lives for our brothers.*" (emphasis added)

Those who follow Jesus are not simply to *tolerate* each other in the name of love or to put on a façade that gives an *appearance* of love as they enter the same building to worship together. Love is not a religious charade but should flow from the heart of a person who has Love Himself indwelling them. If the God who is love is truly leading one of His devoted followers, how could it be otherwise? Love is not simply one of many commandments for those who sincerely want to follow Jesus; it is *the* command.

In fact, Jesus' half brother James called it the *royal* law.[32] It is a stately, ornate, and majestic principle to naturally (or supernaturally) be expressed from those who follow such a loving God. In his letter to the believers in Rome, Paul the Apostle said in Romans 13,

The commandments...are summed up in this one rule: "Love your neighbor as yourself." Love does no harm to its neighbor. Therefore *love is the fulfillment of the law* [i.e., the Old Covenant law of Moses]"

Love was so evident in the early believers, that one historian of the first century wrote, "They love before they know each other."[33]

Their undying commitment to each other was evident to all.

Between scriptures and testimonies from history, this author could record hundreds of times that Christ followers are instructed to love and how the early church did. Okay, let's be real candid. How often have you sensed that level of sacrificial love and acceptance in a local church? As I said earlier, this is where the *rub* is for many.

Let me tell you about a young man who came through my youth ministry. Let's call him Bill, though it is not his real name. Bill was the most rebellious young person I encountered and, in terms of people, was the biggest challenge of my entire twelve-plus years of youth ministry. He grew up with a very godly mom whose atheist husband left her with three kids when she decided to follow Jesus. Bill was the youngest. All through the years of attending the Christian school at our church, he professed that once he was the magic age of eighteen and graduated, he was going to do whatever he wanted to. The actions and attitudes he spoke about all those years, he eventually lived out.

Within a few short years after he graduated, he had stopped attending church or having anything to do with the God of his mother. Bill had covered the strict short hair the school demanded with locks that went halfway down his back. His arms were covered with tattoos with everything from little cartoon demons to a picture of Batman. He became an alcoholic, a drug addict, spent some time homeless, and eventually served time in prison. He became quite a wild man, completely wrecked his life, and broke his mother's heart. Many of us who really cared about

Bill logged many hours praying and even fasting, asking God to bring him back into a right relationship with Him. He eventually answered our prayers. I will never forget the day he came back to church.

Granted, he did not look the part of a typical churchgoer, but he came. Those who had prayed for him and truly cared about his well-being were absolutely thrilled. His mother was ecstatic. But not sister baptized-in-vinegar head of the local Pharisee[34] contingency! Of all the people to be parked next to when he got out of the car in all his rebellious look and attire, *Why her?* I wondered. Instead of welcoming this broken, hurting, prodigal son who was trying to make his way back to God, she gave him the religious evil eye and stared down her nose at him. Bill greeted her, looking (and hoping) for some sense of approval that he was finally coming to a church service. She did not welcome him or say anything kind. Instead, all she said was, "Get a haircut!" That's it! No acceptance. No warm words. No smile. Not even a hello. She would have greeted a visiting stranger better than that... *maybe!*

This woman was a church-going, law-abiding citizen for decades. She could quote Bible verses and recite the great hymns and creeds of church history, but shouldn't the people who have been there the longest be the most like Jesus? Does her attitude and response sound like something that should flow from the heart of one who is under the influence of the Jesus of the Bible? He prayed for His murderers as He hung between heaven and earth on a cruel, rugged Roman cross so that Bill and others like him could know His love and forgiveness. Where was the love in this religiously hateful woman? Sadly, this is what many have experienced. Instead of love, they see religion. Instead of acceptance, they see rejection. Instead of Jesus' love and grace, they see hard faces of disdain.

Since love is so clearly the very heart and essence of God, why are so many in the local church, who are supposed to represent

Him, so critical, harsh, and judgmental? Why so much pious snobbery toward those who may not fit a particular congregation's preconceived ideas about what a Christian is, so much of which is not based on the Bible but pop theology? Even between each other, professing believers battle over such petty things as the style of music used for "worship"; what time religious services should start and end; what kind of snacks should be served in the nursery...on and on it goes. Whenever I hear someone talking about a church fight I think, "Isn't that an oxymoron?"

Lawsuits between believers, divorces over "irreconcilable differences," power struggles for position in church government—these things are common now and all from people who claim to be trying to imitate Jesus! One can hardly help but echo Tina Turner's words, "What's love got to do with it?" Sadly, many people's encounter with church or religious people would make them conclude, *not much*!

In the first letter to the Corinthians, chapter 13, which has become known as the "love chapter," the Apostle Paul described love in these plain terms:

> Love is *patient*, love is *kind*. It *does not envy*, it *does not boast*, it *is not proud*. It *is not rude*, it *is not self-seeking*, it *is not easily angered*, it *keeps no record of wrongs*. Love *does not delight in evil* but *rejoices with the truth*. It always *protects*, always *trusts*, always *hopes*, always *perseveres*. Love *never fails*." (emphasis added)

Is love by this biblical definition really what is most important in the church world?

Many seem to feel as if keeping the rules, showing up at most weekly church meetings, wearing proper church clothes, quoting Bible verses, giving money, and complying with whatever is asked of you are what's important to the church. Love? Isn't it supposed to be *unconditional* if it comes from the God of the Bible? If it's present at all, it's in the minority and only toward those who look and act like them already. Is that really love? In the Sermon on the Mount in Matthew chapter 5 verses 46–47, Jesus talked about conditional love.

> If you love those who love you, what reward will you get? Are not even the tax collectors doing that? And if you greet only your brothers, what are you doing more than others? Do not even pagans do that?

In other words, if professing followers of Christ only accept and love those who are just like them, how are they any different than nonbelievers? They aren't. I received *that* kind of love and more when I hung out in nightclubs and bars in my pre-Christian days! What's love got to do with it? Good question, Tina!

WHERE'S THE BEEF?
(POWERLESSNESS)

The Wendy's commercial was officially entitled "Fluffy Bun" and it aired in January of 1984. Three elderly ladies were seen at the counter of a burger joint and presented with an oversized bun, which naturally drew their attention. Their excited comments on the airy roll turned to disdain when they lifted the top part of the bun revealing a small burger, which barely filled half of the huge roll. One of the ladies, actress Clara Peller, angrily interrupted the discussion with the piercing question, "Where's the beef?" She became more agitated as she repeated the question directed at whoever served it with no reply from behind the counter.[35]

The phrase, "Where's the beef?" became very popular back then and has resurfaced recently in commercials for Wendy's. The phrase questions the substance, validity, and quality of a claim, service, or product. In other words, it raises doubts if what is alleged, asserted, or offered is really accurate. Does it deliver what it professes, or does one experience the old bait and switch? Is the quality or substance of something really there, or are there a lot of bells and whistles, slick advertising, or smoke screens, which when pushed aside, reveal...not much? Again, this is what many experience in the church world. The appearance is that most churchgoers' spiritual experience would alter the words of the well-known hymn "Amazing Grace" to read:

> Mediocre grace,
> How bland the sound,
> That slightly corrected a misguided person like me.
> I once was a little off track,
> But I'm movin' on,
> I had a problem with my eye sight,
> But I got contacts. [36]

Not much power, mediocre, lukewarm, insipid—you get the point.

Clearly, as one reviews the pages of holy writ, one thing is abundantly clear: the God of the Bible is a god of power and might. He is not just mighty, He is "all mighty." He does not just know a lot, He knows everything there is to know. There is no problem, issue, or condition that He cannot change instantaneously if He so desires. A look at biblical history reveals that He very often did. A sound study of scripture shows very plainly, He still wants very much to do such things and is quite able.

In Malachi chapter 3, God was dealing with the fair-weathered devotion of His people and how they were taking advantage of His grace. Their allegiance to Him seemed to be one of convenience and comfort. In other words, as long as they liked what God wanted, as long as it was convenient and did not interfere with their comfort level, plans, or desires, they did it. Is it just me, or does that sound like the majority of professing Christians in America?

The Lord began His convicting words to them with a statement that severely contrasted their character with His. In Malachi 3:6, he said, "I the LORD do not change." Who God is, His intentions for His people and mankind in general has never strayed. The theme of the Bible from Adam and Eve's original sin bringing its consequences into the human race is the same—the redemption of human beings. He wants a restored relationship reestablishing His original design for close, intimate friendship with the only beings created in His image.[37]

This is the same God who created the planets, stars, and the innumerable galaxies of creation just by speaking the word. He created the seasons, the orbits of our solar system, the majestic mountains, unfathomable oceans, and wondrous beauty of all that exists in just six days![38] This is the God who spoke to Moses from a burning bush and then prepared him to deliver His people out of Egyptian bondage. This is the same God who parted the mighty Red Sea to lead two to three million of His chosen people out of over four centuries of slavery across dry ground no less! He then made the waters come crashing down on pharaoh and his army, destroying Israel's enemies.[39]

He's the same God who brought down the walls of Jericho to bring His people into the land He had promised their ancestors generations earlier.[40] These walls were impenetrable by any human means. Jericho was surrounded by two walls—the outer being six feet wide and the inner wall being twelve feet wide.[41] According to history, once Joshua and his people followed God's directions, those mighty walls "fell down, while no instrument of war, nor any other force, was applied to it by the Hebrews."[42]

The Bible and history itself is replete with accounts of Jehovah God's acts of power and might. The greatest of all was the resurrection of His Son Jesus Christ. That event summed up the earthly life and three-hundred-plus prophecies about Him most of which were foretold centuries before He was even born. What other man foretold His own death, the method of that death, burial, and resurrection as well as what day it would happen and then appeared to over five-hundred witnesses at one time to prove it?[43]

The God of the Bible is so unlimited in His power, wisdom, and insight and so amazing in all He is, does and has done that to try to recount all His miraculous and astounding deeds of power would fill more pages than we could count. Yet as one enters the doors of the typical American church and compares the power of this God they profess against all that, well, how could they not notice the immeasurable chasm between the two? The religious services that are supposed to connect one with that same God appear to many seekers as more of a well-timed, meticulously structured religious business meeting than an encounter with Him.

They hear of prayer requests and personal needs brought to this God, yet the vast majority appear to gain no supernatural response and so He seems quite disinterested. Many moments of prayer sound more like a wish list from disheartened people, hoping God will just do something, anything to help them, yet He appears to do little. Compare that to sermons about moving mountains by faith and quotes of "nothing [being] impossible to him who believes," and the incongruity becomes obvious to anyone honest enough to admit it. Reports of church members' marriages disintegrating, struggles with overeating, smoking, pornography, and other life-controlling issues suggests that these religious people have little more power, if any, than their irreligious counterparts. How can any sincere seeker avoid asking, "Where's the beef?"

While believers can respond with truths about God's timing, His will and sovereignty, Christians still have to honestly admit that there is a Grand Canyon of sorts between the displays of power in scripture and the typical church experience today. It's true that power is not the main thing people should seek after, yet what draws most people to pursue God is a need for His help in their powerless condition. Anyone who has experienced the grace of God and His resurrection power knows full well that that same God is alive and well and working His perfect plans.

True as that may be, the cold, hard reality is that most of what occurs in religious services seems birthed in the heart of frail humanity far more than a fresh breathe of inspiration from God.

Those who search for inspiration and divine intervention in their seemingly powerless and mundane existence conclude that the level of what they receive in church gatherings is no more than what they receive at other venues. Sadly, they return to those places from which they came (bars, fortune-tellers, psychic, tarot cards, etc.) allocating their thoughts about church to the "tried that and it didn't work" file in their brains.

IRRELEVANCE NEVER FORGETS! (IRRELEVANCE)

Growing up was tough in the seventies, and I am certain it is no easier today. In fact, in many ways, it is much more difficult. The issues people young and old grapple with today were not even on the radar screen those decades ago. At that time, who even considered matters like the incredibly easy access and seemingly shame-free accessibility to pornography? Things like gender-confusion, human cloning, physician-assisted suicide, partial-birth abortion, and a multitude of other conundrums were not in the forefront at that time, or even on the back burner, for that matter!

Besides the usual struggles of peer pressure, high divorce rates, racing hormones, and academic pressures, younger people today face matters of vicious gangs, school shootings, and sophisticated "designer" drugs at levels never addressed by their parents and grandparents. With all those things on the horizon and often part of their daily lives, when they are seeking divine aid, the asserting of religious truths must have some clear connection to their life's issues. In other words, it must be *relevant*, or it will simply be put to the side or dismissed from their ideology.

CHURCH! WHO NEEDS IT?!

The message of the gospel of Jesus Christ is always relevant. Always! It is timeless and transcends all issues of humanity. However, the way it is *packaged* or presented is often *not* relevant. One thing that seems clear is that a person or persons must accept the messenger before they accept the message. When I was converted and Jesus radically changed my life, something that really caught my attention was how it impacted the life of the young man who presented it to me. Also, his likeness to me both in his pre-Christian and (then) present days, his goals in life, his personality, as well as the manner in which he presented that message produced a sense of connection in me. *What* he was saying and *how* he said it seemed like it would really matter, not only when I died but in my daily life. In my prior religious and church experience, that is precisely what was missing in the equation. All the stained glass, rituals, and piety did not seem to provide anything that would make any difference in my daily life. I felt no sense of connection, and thus, the truths asserted seemed irrelevant. I have discovered that my experience is not unique. Still today, many see the church as irrelevant to "real" life. Yet with such a significant, life-altering, destiny-changing message, one cannot help but ask why?

The American Heritage Dictionary defines *relevance* as something that shows "pertinence to the matter at hand" or has "applicability to social issues."[44] When an idea, practice, product, or approach is relevant, it means there is a connection between it and the need at hand. In terms of spiritual pursuits, it would mean that what is being asserted and even *how* it is being projected connects the audience with the need at hand—that there is a way to apply it all to one's situation or circumstances. If the gospel of Jesus Christ does not fit that definition, I have not even the slightest clue what does!

In regards to relevance, I share the following real-life and twentieth-century example of one man and his rags-to-riches venture. Ray Croc was the founder of a five-spindled machine that made milk shakes. He heard about a food store that was using five of them at one time in California and headed out to see it for himself. What he saw amazed him as he had never seen such frantic activity to serve so many customers at one time. He suggested to the two brothers running the burger stand that they consider opening up other stores. One of the brothers wondered whom they would get to run them, and Mr. Croc said he would gladly do it.

The year was 1954, and Croc was fifty-two years old. He opened the first one in Des Plaines, Illinois, and the first day's revenue was a whopping $366.12. Today, the chain that blossomed from that little burger stand is the most well-known restaurant in the entire world. It "is the leading global foodservice retailer with more than 30,000 local restaurants serving 52 million people in more than 100 countries each day." Those two brothers, Dick and Mac McDonald could never have imagined what would come from their little venture and agreement with McDonald's founder Ray Croc.[45] Yet as I ponder the product, I cannot help but ask why?

Please understand, I do not mean that their food is bad, but is it really that special that it should bring in billions of dollars in income every year and become a world-renowned icon? McDonald's took a mediocre product, advertised it heavily, and priced it relatively inexpensive so most people could afford it. Add to that playgrounds, games, and toys to attract children, as well as wrapping it in flashy packages while making it all quick and easy and, behold, a star is born! McDonald's was and continues to be *relevant* to the average American's life. There is a connection from their product and service to the fast-paced family life so prevalent in our culture. To apply this to the church and her *product*, so to speak, it seems to me that we believers have done the exact opposite. Let me explain.

We have taken the most powerful, important, relevant *product*, if you will, and have insisted that our society bend to how we have *packaged* it. The gospel of Jesus Christ, backed by the life-changing power of the Holy Spirit and all the principles of the Bible, holds the most relevant truths that have or ever will exist. Those truths transcend time and culture even as the God who gave us them does. Let me clarify that I am not suggesting that the message be altered or watered down in any way. However, while the *message* must never change, the *methods* must *always* be under scrutiny. Believers can only hope to connect that message with its audience by adjusting those methods.

With all that in mind, consider these questions. Now before you read them, if you are someone entrenched in the typical church culture of our society, you may want to pray because they will challenge your thinking. Okay, here we go. Why do so many churches use worship music that is literally decades out-of-date? Please understand, I am not referring to hymns rich with scriptural truths often forged in the fires of adversity by the spiritual giants of the past. However, why do they have to keep the same tempo in a culture whose most popular music has moved away from that many, many years ago? Surely, those truths would not lose their impact because the rhythm is changed, would they?

If the audience is more from that time era, then certainly, keeping that tempo makes it more relevant to *those* people. However, since 85 percent of people who come to personal, genuine faith in Christ do so before eighteen years of age, does that not suggest that the majority of non-Christians, truth-seekers, and backsliders could not relate to such music? How relevant would it seem to younger people, who hardly even know what us baby boomers mean by the words *vinyl album* or *eight-track*, when that same music is presented through a pipe organ and no modern instruments whatsoever? Many churchgoers, especially those who grew up attending religious services, want to keep the old stuff simply because it arouses sentiments from their earlier years. Yet if we're trying to reach people who have little or even no church background, is arousing emotions of long-time believers really that important?

Here is more to ponder. Does anyone really read a church bulletin? If so, why do so many ask questions that are clearly already answered in that publication? Why do so few people *read* a gospel tract when it is given to them, particularly from someone they do not know? The answer? People born before the modern era of communications (cell phones, e-mail, iPods, etc.) were used to *printed* materials. Those are typically the only people who connect with church bulletins, tracts, and other such modes of communication. Yet something as simple and seemingly irrelevant has become a sacred cow in many congregations. Why?

Friend, there a many more examples that could be written here, but the point is, the way the love of God is presented must connect with those to whom it is addressed. With the number of unchurched people in America growing faster than the population, it is apparent that that connection is not occurring. Why do so many churchgoers refuse to see this and then wonder why their church does not reach more people?

Now that I have already brought up things that would upset the typical religious person, why not press a little further? In the New Testament, the word used particularly by Jesus' close friend John to describe the godless system of this world is the word *worldly*. It defines the typical pattern of either neglecting or rejecting (which is really the same thing) the God of the Bible and his teachings. Sadly, many in the church world have deemed modern modes of communication and presentation as *worldly* with no biblical basis whatsoever. Because of that, their attempts to be relevant have failed miserably. They are more concerned with what other religious people think than what God actually says in his word. God states no preference to styles of music, fashion[46] (casual or business attire), time of day for religious services, having a Sunday night religious service. Yet somehow many of these things have become so ingrained in a congregation's DNA they have become more important than actually affecting the lives of hurting human beings. Again, must we not ask, why?

Know this. For the glorious gospel of Jesus Christ to impact a seeker, though the message must never change, it must be presented in a way that is relevant to that person. Believers will spend much time and money to send missionaries to other lands and cultures to bring that gospel to people who do not know this loving, gracious God. Does this not beg the question, why do so many churchgoers struggle with doing that right here in our own country? To send them overseas, we often view discovering a relevant approach to presenting the gospel as necessary, vital, and indispensable. Why should it be any different here on our own soil? We must understand that any seeker who enters the doors of a local congregation must sense that relevance, or they will dismiss the greatest news of all time, and that is eternally tragic beyond description!

MR. AND MRS. GOOD ENOUGH (LACK OF EXCELLENCE)

Like most families, ours longed to take our kids to the greatest and most fun place on earth, particularly for children. We may have been able to vacation at Disney in Orlando, Florida, sooner had we made it a top priority; however, we thought it best to wait until our three sons were old enough to both enjoy and remember the experience. So we scratched, skimped, and saved for two years and finally spent the fortune necessary to go to, as our youngest son calls it, "Mickey's house."

Though I have personally been there several other times, I had never been with my kids. The first time I went was 1982, if memory serves me correctly. In all my visits there, including this one with my wife and sons, I am always amazed at how clean the grounds and attractions are kept. From the well-trimmed hedges shaped as different animals and the spotless sidewalks to the friendliness of the costumed characters to the food courts, the commitment to excellence is crystal clear. Disney considers what they do important enough to do all that they do well, very well. This is a major reason why they are the most well-known and well-attended amusement park on planet Earth.

I wonder what a family would do if they saved all the necessary funds, flew in, checked into a plush hotel off the grounds, got the kids up early, and drove to the park and found everything in shoddy condition? Picture it. They drive down International Drive with each member of the family bursting with anticipation that has been building for however long they were planning the trip. As they drive into the park, instead of finding the usual topnotch grounds and friendly greeters, they see overgrown grass, "out of shape" hedges, and are met by grumpy people in torn jeans and tank tops. The lines to the Monorail are extremely long, but they wait their turn. Their transportation comes after a solid hour of waiting while trying to keep everyone from complaining. Once they get into the park, all the lines are amazingly long because the maintenance team did not prepare the rides on time.

The employees who were to run the rides showed up late because management did not get the work schedule out to them on time, so they had to make last-minute phone calls to get workers there. By noontime, the family had only gotten to ride two rides, so they meet for lunch only to find more long lines. They finally get their burgers, fries, and drinks only to find the hamburger meat was not fully cooked and hard as plastic; the fries are cold and stale; and their Coke is flat. Their vacation was for four days and three nights, and they found the same shoddy workmanship consistently day in and day out, ride after ride.

Obviously, this is just a fictitious example to make a point. Disney's deep commitment to excellence is unmatched, known by all, and inspires those who have vacationed there to return and those who have not been there to be drawn in by the testimonies of those who have. If that commitment to excellence ever wanes so will their attendance along with their revenue.

Now if this fictitious example really took place, do you think that that family would respond with understanding and try to excuse Disney's lack of excellence? When they got back to their regular lives, what do you think they would tell their friends and relatives about their experience? Is the expectation of excellence in the people who attend reasonable? Of course it is! That is what drew them there in the first place. That is what motivated them to save their money and plan to go there. They would be very disappointed and feel cheated if they found it any other way. Is it any different in the local church? I do not believe so.

In one area I ministered in, my family and I would pass by a church that advertised a particular event revolving around a dinner. When we first moved there, it did catch our attention. However, as time sailed by and the event came and went, it was obvious they were not going to update it. In fact, they did not change that sign for eight months until it no longer grabbed our attention but rather aroused irritation.

One church near us during another tenure of ministry changed their sign about four times a year. Such inattention to detail communicates a lack of concern for their "audience." It also implies that they do not count what they are doing as very important. Church signs are just one example of the lack of excellence in many churches.

Let me share another example. The little girl was so cute the congregation just melted when she climbed the stairs to the altar to sing her solo. She and her family were devoted churchgoers and loved by all. There was only one problem: she could not sing. No, no, I mean, she *really* could not sing. I do not want to seem mean, but she was so off-key it was like fingernails down a blackboard. She was a fine young lady (about eleven years old) with a sincere desire to do something for God, but her talents obviously lay elsewhere. So why is she allowed to sing a solo during a religious service? Also why would some consider it unkind to even ask this question? While the people who regularly attend that church and know and love the girl can endure it and even clap for her when she is done, can a visitor? What about someone who is a seeker who has come in search of *truth*?

I once heard a minister say, "If the church does not give them a chance, the world will." He was obviously referring to bars, nightclubs, and other "ungodly" venues. While this is certainly something to think about, the question must be posed, "Do you really think so?" Does anyone really think that secular bands and places of entertainment will give someone who cannot sing well a platform to sing anyway? I doubt it.

Watch an episode of *American Idol,* and you will see the opposite is true. Is it not just common sense that people should operate within the sphere of their gifts and talents? Should this fine young lady not have either been coached with voice lessons until she sang well enough or, if no progress occurred in her voice, kindly directed to express her love for God in another way? Is allowing her to continue to publicly irritate the ears of people who love her setting her up for public humiliation when she tries to use her *talent* before an audience that has no relational connection with her? The answer is obvious. It is deceiving her in the name of love. What a paradox! It is trading truth for an illusion of being *nice.* Also, it tells the visitor (sinner, seeker, or saint) who does not know the girl that whoever was in charge of scheduling the music ministry that morning did not consider excellence to be important.

Does that not tarnish things and give the impression that what is being done in that religious service is not serious enough to present the message in an enjoyable and excellent way? It is true that this girl's effort was beautiful to the God who looks on the heart but man has to endure the physical reality of...well, poor singing!

How about plays and drama? I will never forget a children's event I attended where a skit was done. Every actor and actress carried the book with their lines in front of their faces for all to see as they *read* their lines aloud. To make it worse, they did not even do that with any flare but with monotone voices and little expression of any kind. The props and everything may have been in place, but it would be difficult to classify what they did as acting as there was little (if any) involved. The message was lost because the presentation was of extremely poor quality.

It would be ridiculous to expect adolescents to perform like true professional actors, and that is not what I am suggesting. However, is it too much to ask that they at least know their lines well enough to not carry book in front of them and that they put some expression into it?

A seeker once called the church I ministered in. She had no religious background whatsoever but thought it might be a good thing for their family and especially their two young children. To illustrate how unchurched she was, you should know that the first time they came to a midweek religious service, they dropped off the kids and waited outside in the parking lot for them to be done having no idea there was anything for adults! They had never entered a sanctuary, synagogue, or religious institution of any kind. That is not the astounding part though.

In search of truth, this woman called multiple churches in our town. Only one or two of them even had an answering machine for her to leave a message. Also she never even received a call back from the ones that did. Remember, this was not an isolated incident but the normal responses she received. One minister even got irritated at her over the phone because she asked too many questions!

The examples of poor quality in the religious world I have seen over three decades could fill volumes. Here are some examples—no website or a low-quality one in a day of immense technological advancement; ministers who cannot even be found when people are in crisis; bulletins and other printed material filled with spelling errors; outdated worship music; joyless choirs; shabby buildings; smelly, dirty restrooms; unorganized nurseries;

overgrown lawns and shrubbery; carpet that should have been replaced years ago, and on and on and on.

Why does Disney, the music industry, the business world, and an innumerable number of other secular organizations treat what they do with more commitment to its quality than the church does? While the church may not have the revenue to do all that nonreligious groups often do, surely a commitment to excellence says what they are doing is important. Conversely, a lack of that commitment says the opposite.

Keep in mind, what these other organizations do serves mankind in *temporal* matters of this life. However, what the church has to offer is of so much more value than any of that. The gospel of Jesus Christ impacts this life and the one to come forever. The church's *product*, so to speak, will change a person's destiny from being a hell-raiser to a God praiser. It can restore broken marriages, heal broken hearts, deliver the bound, and do more good to people than all of the nonreligious organizations and efforts *combined*! Certainly, that gospel[47] message should be presented in an excellent manner giving every detail of its expression and the administration thereof *far* more attention and quality effort than anything else in this world!

IS IT AN ALTAR OR A STAGE? (HYPOCRISY)

Of all the complaints people use against organized religion, the one most commonly heard is that of hypocrisy. The word *hypocrite* refers to "a stage actor, hence one who pretends to be what he is not."[48] It is further defined in two similar ways:

1. a person who pretends to have virtues, moral or religious beliefs, principles, etc., that he or she does not actually possess, esp. a person whose actions belie stated beliefs [or]

2. a person who feigns some desirable or publicly approved attitude, esp. one whose private life, opinions, or statements belie his or her public statements.[49]

Unchurched people simply cannot reconcile the idea of someone who professes one thing with their mouth but shows no consistent actions or attitudes that agree with that profession. When the conduct does not match the confession, people question the validity of the belief in the first place. Can anyone really blame them?

It seems important to clarify that a hypocrite is not the same as someone who is sincerely trying to live out what they believe. A hypocrite is basically an insincere actor whether knowingly or not. A churchgoer or spiritual seeker who struggles with sin and human weakness but is truly attempting to please the Lord is not a hypocrite. One who attends religious services and goes through all the seemingly appropriate gestures and uses the acceptable lingo while they are there and yet none (or little) of those things are present the rest of their daily life is an actor on a stage. They are putting on a performance. Whether to salve their own conscience, please a family member, earn points with God (who already loves them deeply, by the way) or to be seen as a good citizen, if it isn't from the heart, the person is a hypocrite.

An altar is a place of sacrifice and dedication and a place of submission to and worship of one deemed as a divine entity. If one lives their life and all they do as done on an altar, though they will struggle with their humanity, they view their efforts—as feeble as they may be—as worship. A good way to know one's sincerity level can be seen in a person's reaction to the truth of their belief system. In other words, if I say I believe that the God of the Bible is my God, what is my response to His instructions or directions in that sacred book of how I am to worship Him? If I say I agree with what He says about the importance of prayer yet just sort of *squeeze* prayer in when it is most convenient for me and all my own desires, am I on an altar or a stage?

Let me make a jarring statement: guilt is underrated. Though it can be used as a tool to manipulate or control, it is also a God-ordained instrument to help guide humanity. For instance, if I do something that I know goes against what I believe God wants of me, I *should* feel guilty. If I have intentionally violated what I know is right and true and yet I feel no guilt, that is a *major* problem. Similarly, if the Bible, the guidebook for the Christ-follower, says I am to do or *not* do something and I know it yet refuse to align myself with it, in what sense am I following the Lord? I am not and am simply keeping up a front. I am on a stage, not an altar.

Though sincerity can only truly be seen by God, it is safe to agree with so many who proclaim, so far as humanity can tell, the church is full of hypocrites—people who profess they believe in the power and absolute necessity of prayer yet hardly pray and make every excuse in the world to avoid attending prayer services. Others say they believe people who die without Jesus as their Lord go to an eternal place of torment yet make little attempt to obey the Lord's clear commands to tell others how to avoid that awful place. Many want Jesus as their savior to rescue them from any place of punishment but resist him as their Lord and master because they still want to be in control; basically, they still want to rule their lives and be their own god. It is quite telling that the word *savior* always follows the word *lord* when referring to Christ in the New Testament. That is simply because he cannot be a person's savior without being his or her lord *first*. The old saying is, "If he's not Lord *of* all, He isn't Lord *at* all."

I heard a story told once of a minister who was invited to speak at a gathering of other ministers. The good reverend, knowing the pressures, stresses, and discouragements of the ministry, spent much time praying and preparing to be an encouragement to that group. As he drove to check into his hotel before going to the meeting place, he was about to pass a car on the highway, and he noticed a "Christian" bumper sticker. It read, "Honk if you love

Jesus." The minister felt he fit the category, so he beeped his horn as he was driving by. The driver's reaction was very unexpected. He waved, but it was with a backward peace sign minus one finger!

The speaker was upset but calmed himself down and checked into his hotel to freshen up before the meeting. Imagine his reaction as he spotted that very same car in the parking lot where he was about to be the main speaker! He came to the pulpit and told the story to the entire assembly. We can only imagine the shocked faces (and one of them beet red) as he advised whoever minister was driving that car to remove his bumper sticker as soon as possible and change his conduct. Amen! In essence, from the altar, this speaker challenged that minister to get off the stage and get back on the altar. Be genuine. Be real. Be a true lover of God.

Who could forget the various public scandals of fallen religious leaders that we've heard about throughout the years? Thankfully, the exposure of all the hypocrisy in men's lives can be a tool in the hand of a gracious God to bring them back to genuine godliness. You see, if one is a genuine child of God, staying on the stage too long causes the loving God of the Bible to orchestrate circumstances meant to put you back where you belong—on the altar.

WOLVES IN THE HENHOUSE (SEXUAL PREDATORS)

Part of my upbringing as a Roman Catholic was a deep respect for "men of the cloth." We were taught that such men are God's representatives and just one step away from the Lord himself. To be close to a priest was to be close to God. I served as an altar boy from about ten to twelve years old. When my parents left me with a priest, they hadn't a worry in the world concerning my well-being. I doubt that even the idea that such a man of God would ever take advantage of that trust to expend his own sinfulness upon me ever entered their minds. Thankfully, no priest ever violated that trust in my life. And before I write on, let me say that the vast majority of priests and ministers never do. Those clergy who do such evil to children are a rare exception, but the tragedy is that there are those who will.

I can still picture the face of one priest on the television screen when he was confronted by his victims decades after the fact. He became angry and basically attacked the cameraman. It was a news show like *Primetime*. They even recorded the conversation one victim had with him by phone asking him why he took advantage of him as a child. The priest said he didn't know why but that he had since gotten help for his problem. More and more victims began to surface from that one priest. Shortly thereafter, they seemed to be coming out of the woodwork. Victims all across the country felt empowered to finally talk about their suffering as children at the hands of clergyman.

During my time at Bible College, I had the honor and privilege of sitting under the tutelage of the leading legal authority from a religious perspective, Dr. Richard Hammar. Have you ever taken a class that you felt you needed but honestly expected it to be a lesson in boredom? Such is how I felt when I took the class Pastor and Law at Central Bible College in Springfield, Missouri. Well, Dr. Hammar had such a way of presenting the material and leading the class that it turned out to be my best experience of all the classes I have ever taken. It was revealing, interesting, and amazingly shocking all at the same time.

Dr. Hammar has literally written volumes on cases he has to deal with involving church lawsuits and the like. I sat astounded and disgusted as he shared case after case of children being violated by their most trusted leaders. From clergymen to boy's group's leaders to sleepovers, and much more, the cases were many and incredibly tragic.

Can you imagine? The place a child should be the safest turned out to be the place they were in the most danger. As a parent of three boys, one of them with multiple special needs, I cannot imagine the sense of betrayal those parents, not to mention those children, must have felt. The question must then be posed, what does such an experience do to a person's view of God? Does a child then see God as a big bully who only wants to use him or her for His own desires and toss them aside? Many who have been molested by a representative of the church (whether a clergy member or lay leader) struggle with seeing the God of the Bible as the loving Father He truly is. Of course, this is certainly understandable and tragic!

How does God view such violations of little ones? Consider the words of Jesus in the gospel of Matthew, "But whoso shall offend one of these little ones which believe in Me, it were better for him that a millstone were hanged about his neck, and that he were drowned in the depth of the sea" (Matthew 18:6, KJV).

In another situation, parents wanted this great teacher and prophet who had been healing and helping so many to simply touch their kids. The attitudes of his apostles compared to His own are revealing as to how Jesus feels about children. Consider these words from the tenth chapter of Mark's gospel,

> "People were bringing little children to Jesus to have Him touch them, but the disciples rebuked them. When Jesus saw this, *he was indignant*. He said to them, "Let the little children come to Me, and do not hinder them, for the kingdom of God belongs to such as these. I tell you the truth, anyone who will not receive the kingdom of God like a little child will never enter it.' And He took the children in his arms, put His hands on them *and blessed them*." [emphasis added]

"Indignant!" The New King James Bible uses the words *greatly displeased* to describe Jesus' feelings. However, the New Living Translation seems to carry it best as simply *angry*. Jesus was ticked off, hot under the collar, ready to blow his stack or whatever phrase one might use to describe a state of hot and furious emotion. The fact that He stated earlier that offenders of children would be better off drowned with a big rock around their neck, well, it's quite clear how He feels about the molesters! Can He forgive them and redeem them? Of course He can, but they still do not belong close to their area of sick desire—children. Also, the ripple effects from their twisted behavior in the lives of their victims can literally ruin them for life. No wonder He hates such behavior, it harms those beings He cherishes the most—people, particularly children!

Thus far, we have primarily looked at cases involving children. Sadly, cases involving sexual predators do not stop there. How many clergymen have taken advantage of women they have counseled? Vulnerable, hurting, and in desperate need of love and affection, many a female has fallen prey to the groping hands of a minister, priest, or rabbi. How incredibly sad!

With all that in mind, how do these situations impact the mind of one looking for truth and for God? Further, how would they affect those who themselves were taken advantage of sexually in their past? Surely, they would be hesitant, at the very least, to darken the door of such an institution and put themselves and their children at risk.

Of all places, leaders at religious institutions need to be vigilant and maybe even *militant* at doing all they can to be sure their people are as safe as humanly possible. A predator may be able to get past safeguards, but these barriers still need to be put firmly in place!

MORE THAN MORE-THAN CONQUERORS (POWER MONGERS)

In the mid-1980s, I was privileged to travel with the pastor I served under, as well as several other leaders, to a nationally known minister's conference in New Orleans. Leaders traveled from all across the nation and even from other countries to gain the insights that would make them more effective pastors. The teaching and messages were insightful and encouraging, and the worship was overwhelmingly inspiring. However, my most vivid memory of that trip is not very spiritual.

We had a day off in that week to travel around the city and see the sights. I'll never forget (though I've tried!) some of the sights I saw on Bourbon Street in the French Quarter. It seemed obvious that there were plenty of people who need hope and help. In our travels that day, we stopped to take some pictures by the river. Some of the men struck up a conversation with a troubled soul who was begging and appeared to be homeless. They were trying to tell him about the hope that Jesus had brought into their lives and assuring him that the same hope was available to him. In that discussion, the man began to talk about some of his sexual struggles and asked a couple of questions in that vein. I'll never forget my pastor's reaction.

In a clear expression of disgust for this beggar, our fearless leader loudly told us to just get away from him and commented on how he was wasting our time. Predictably, the man responded in like called my pastor back as he was walking away. He immediately turned around, walked up to the beggar, and got nose-to-nose with him. The man asked, "You're a man, aren't you?" Basically implying he must have some kind of similar struggles, if he would be totally transparent.

Looking down his "holier than thou" nose, the pastor replied, "Yes, but I'm also a preacher, and I don't like that kind of talk." He then waved us on and led us all away from this hurting man.

I remember feeling shocked as we walked away, and I wondered if any of the other men felt the same way. Here we were, a bunch of spiritual leaders who traveled well over a thousand miles and spent thousands of dollars to attend a conference to help us minister to hurting people more effectively, yet our leader just confronted a lost soul who simply seemed to have some sincere questions about how he would deal with his sexuality if he decided

to follow the savior that we were telling him about! Instead of
giving him the truth and love he was searching for, this pastor
intimidated him into silence. What's wrong with this picture?

Over time, this man's need for power and domination became
clear. I watched him bully and intimidate anyone who dared to
disagree with him. He consistently assassinated the character of
anyone who voiced any deviation from his views or ways. This
was subtly done by couching his slanderous words about them in
spiritual phrases and then telling people they should *pray* for the
person he was backbiting. This gave the appearance that he really
cared about their supposed struggle when the truth was he was
using that weakness to leverage his authority over them in hopes
they would eventually either cower into submission or leave his
church. That would allow him to remain the top dog and still be
in control. Over the years, I realized that what happened in New
Orleans was just the tip of the iceberg and only one example of
many. This same man carried a .357 Magnum under the seat of
the vehicle he drove! He obviously had a problem with power.

Sadly, he is not alone. After decades of ministry involvement,
I could share many more cases of people (not just pastors) power
posturing to intimidate and bully people. Instead of many, I'll
share just one.

Pete (not his real name) had been a long-standing member
of the church, served as a deacon for several terms, and had a
Sunday school class he taught for twenty years. A local business
owner and family man, most everyone liked and looked up to
him. He was typically gracious, generous, and easy to talk to as
long as everything went his way and the person he was interact-
ing with did not carry any authority (real or perceived) over him.
As the self-appointed overseer of the pastor, he had a history
of verbally assaulting the lead minister of that church. I interviewed the pastor who served before me and, though he affirmed
Pete's potential to be a blessing, he also warned me about his
track record.

Feeling as though effectiveness to reach and mentor people for Jesus was my primary concern, I always tried to discover the best way to see that accomplished. As is in the typical church of the Western world, the primary focus of this congregation was almost exclusively inward. As long as the long-standing attendees were content and some "good things" were happening, there was little true concern about those outside our doors who may not know the savior. Our midweek service and the accompanying ministries all reflected that.

Change comes slowly and with resistance for most people, but even more so for long-standing church members who have invested much of their time and resources in that church. Human nature is to get settled into a routine that makes us the most comfortable and costs us the least inconvenience. Sadly, in the church world, that can equate to marginalizing or even losing the mission for which Jesus established his church on earth, reaching and mentoring people to follow Him.

In an effort to discover how to improve our effectiveness for our midweek ministries, I met with our leadership team for the next year and a half—eighteen months. During that time, we prayed, discussed, debated, read books, and decided *together* to implement a small home group ministry. Before that decision was finalized, we took a secret vote (only I was looking) and fourteen of the fifteen leaders in the room agreed that this was what we needed to do. Pete was one of the fourteen.

He was voted onto the board of deacons during my tenure at this particular church, so he was a major part of all the decision-making and approval for funds, as well as everything the process required. With that high percentage of unity, the direction was clear. So we decided to set a meeting for the whole church to come together so we could tell them what we had decided and to answer any concerns they had. Then it happened. On the day of the meeting, I made the mistake of sending out an e-mail to some of our workers that Pete didn't like.

We all have events in our lives that so impact us that we can remember exactly where we were when they occurred. Well, what followed is one of those in my life. It was literally two minutes before what was to be one of the most important meetings and ministry shifts during my time there. I was standing in the foyer greeting people as they came in. The excitement level was high, though there was definitely some apprehension for some of the older members.

Then Pete walked up. He said to me, "That e-mail you sent today really flipped a switch in me. Up to this point, I've been your supporter. But from this point on, I will not be, and I am going to oppose what we're doing here tonight." Then he simply walked into the sanctuary where the meeting was to take place, where he was warmly greeted by everyone who knew him so well. To say I was shaken up would be the understatement of a lifetime.

Before that encounter, I had no reason to believe that he or any other leader was in opposition to what we had decided *together*. This church had six decades of history. This man had been there for one-third of that, and I was the new guy with less than two years there. I hardly knew how to proceed. I was angry. I was hurt. I was bewildered. I was tongue-tied and nervous.

True to his threat, he stood up and basically called me a liar as the whole team sat in shock knowing full well that he had given approval for each step of this process. Though his goal was to bully me, he was actually coming against the whole team—that didn't matter to him. His lack of support carried ripple effects that hindered that church's growth and effectiveness for the next two years.

There were multiple other incidences that I have not written here. This one was just the final volcanic eruption from one who had come to be known as the *church bully*, especially toward the pastor. Like a spoiled brat that picks up his ball and goes home so the other kids cannot do what he does not want them to, he eventually resigned all his positions and left the church.

Some of the things he said and did during these moments of tension made both my wife and me cry. He was the cause of many sleepless nights and tension-filled days. I almost left the church, and it would have taken very little prompting from God to get me to. Positions gave Pete a sense of power and, at that time, he somehow did not understand that roles in the church are about humble service to others, not wielding power to get your way.

What a stark contrast to the savior these men and all Christ followers are to represent! Power-mongers need to dominate people instead of serving them as Jesus did. The scary part is that, in the church, they often do that while using scripture and spiritual-sounding words that can make it all seem like the will of God to the one unskilled in handling the Bible accurately!

The writer of the first gospel in the New Testament penned these tender words of Jesus in Matthew chapter 11 verses 28–30,

> Come to me, all you who are weary and burdened, and I will give you rest. Take my yoke upon you and learn from me, for *I am gentle and humble in heart*, and you will find rest for your souls. For my yoke is easy and my burden is light. (Emphasis added)

Humility should characterize those who follow the humble Christ.

One of Jesus' early followers, the Apostle Paul wrote these words in a letter to some Christ followers in the city of Philippi centuries ago:

> Your attitude should be the same as that of Christ Jesus: Who, being in very nature God, did not consider equality with God something to be grasped, *but made Himself nothing*, taking the very nature of a servant, being made in human likeness. And being found in appearance as a man, *He humbled Himself* and became obedient to death—even death on a cross [emphasis added]![50]

Jesus won hurting people over through His love, grace, and mercy, not by trying to bully or intimidate them. And let's face it. As the Son of God, He had the power to intimidate anyone! Yet His harshest words were never for the *hurting* or what some might term the unlovable. No, He reserved those for the professing *religious* people of His time. They were professing to be one thing, representing the God of heaven, but Jesus saw right through them. He declared, "⁷ You hypocrites! Isaiah [an Old Testament prophet] was right when he prophesied about you: ⁸ These people honor Me with their lips, *but their hearts are far from Me* [emphasis added]."

The words *church* and *bully* should never be in the same sentence! However, since religious gatherings are only made up of imperfect people (which includes all of us), there will always be people who feel the need to dominate and control others. Friend, if you have been bullied by someone who was supposed to represent the humble Christ of the Bible, I can tell you, I know how that feels. I can also tell you, at least in those instances, they were not accurately portraying the God of the Bible. With God's help, you can avoid projecting their poor example of Jesus on Him or His followers.

A THIEF IN THE LIGHT (SWINDLERS)

There is a reason that thieves rarely strike during daylight. The probability of their actions being exposed is far greater than if they occurred in the evening. Jesus' close friend John⁵¹ spoke of this as well in the third chapter of his gospel. In referring to Jesus' entrance into this world, he wrote,

> ¹⁹ Here is the verdict; Light has come into the world, but men loved darkness instead of light because their deeds were evil. Everyone who does evil hates the light, and will not come into the light for fear that his deeds will be exposed."

Jesus also referred to Himself as "the Light of the World."[52]
The New Testament explains that to have a close relationship with Jesus is to walk in (or with) the light.

In his letter to the Christ followers in the city of Thessalonica, the Apostle Paul described the tone of Jesus' return. In writing to these believers, he said, "For you know very well that the day of the Lord will come like a thief in the night."[53] Is it just me, or does it seem rather strange to compare the return of the holy Son of God with the sudden unexpected entrance of a criminal?

Well, consider, how *does* a thief come? They do not typically call ahead to warn their victim, do they? Can you imagine? Your phone rings, you answer. A deep raspy voice on the other end says, "Uh...yeah...this is Mr. Thug...I just wanted to let you know that me and my boys have been watching your family's movements for about six weeks. We've pinned down the time we're coming to rob you...it will be about two thirty Thursday morning...will that work for you, guys?"

Shocked but grateful, you would tell him that would be fine. Then you would call the local police who would stealthily watch your house till that Thursday. Then they would set up shop in your house the night before. Mr. Thug and his cohorts would show up in the wee hours of Thursday morning and promptly be arrested. All the time in between his phone call and their robbery attempt, you would be at ease. Why? Because you knew the exact time of their arrival. Ridiculous? Absurd? Of course it is! That's the point exactly.

Jesus' friend Matthew records something He said along these lines in the twenty-fourth chapter of his gospel. He was explaining to them about the suddenness of the savior's second coming and the need for being prepared. He said, "But understand this: If the owner of the house had known at what time of night the thief was coming, he would have kept watch and would not have let his house be broken into."[54]

Again, this is an allusion to sudden unexpected return of Christ when He quickly removes His followers from this world (often referred to as the *rapture* meaning, "quick removal"). He will come and steal His people away without warning or notice, just like a thief.

One does not expect a thief in the *light* but in the *night*. That combined with the fact that God's people, particularly His leaders, are called to live a holy life,[55] finding people in church leadership who essentially rob those they are called to lovingly guide is shocking. The followers of Jesus are expected to "walk in the light as He [Jesus] is in the light."[56] This means to live a life that is pleasing to God, like Jesus modeled. Christ followers speak of living holy and the leaders especially espouse a lifestyle reminiscent of their master. So how is it that the church world has so many swindlers in it? Good question! Let me give you an example of swindling in the "light."

*   *   *

To say that James Randi is a skeptic of the supernatural would be quite an understatement. His website describes him as follows:

> James Randi has an international reputation as a magician and escape artist, but today he is best known as the world's most tireless investigator and demystifier of paranormal and pseudoscientific claims.
>
> Randi has pursued "psychic" spoonbenders, exposed the dirty tricks of faith healers, investigated homeopathic water "with a memory," and generally been a thorn in the sides of those who try to pull the wool over the public's eyes in the name of the supernatural.[57]

Affirming those comments above, he is known for investigating claims of supernatural powers of any kind. In this regard, he is most noted for exposing the trickery of alleged psychic Uri

Geller. Unbeknownst to Geller, Johnny Carson called on Randi's expertise in an attempt to test his alleged skills. To say the least, Geller was publicly embarrassed when he could not do his usual spoon-bending demonstration of his psychic powers. The reason his alleged powers failed is that Randi directed *The Tonight Show* staff to provide Geller with their own spoons and other items for him to assert those supposed powers on. Of course, Geller could not and claimed that he simply did not feel "strong" in his powers that night. Randi eventually shared his discoveries and views in the book he wrote entitled, *The Truth About Uri Geller*.

In the 1980s, Randi had no qualms about entering the world of professing faith healers. In his pursuits, he focused on one particular healing evangelist by the name of Peter Popoff.[58] Thousands were attending his healing crusade meetings and professing a divine touch during them. Randi felt what he was doing simply seemed a little *too* divine and had to have some kind of rational explanation.

Popoff would walk around the audience and call out the names of people he had never met. He would then tell the person's address, ailment, and other personal issues he could not have known on his own. Randi decided to take a radio frequency scanner into one of his crusades. What was finally revealed was the Popoff was wearing a small wireless speaker in his ear while his wife read the information off of prayer cards that people had filled out before the meeting. I still remember seeing a news show that exposed Popoff for the phony swindler he really was. The amazing thing to me was Popoff's response when confronted with the truth. He simply said that he was just using modern technology to advance the cause of Christ and had done nothing wrong! According to Randi, not long after all this was made public, Popoff went from a four million dollar annual income to having to claim bankruptcy. In my opinion, he should have gone to prison for fraud and putting false hope into the hearts of innocent God-fearing people.

Sadly, this man is still in ministry today. His website says,

> "Rev. Peter Popoff, People United For Christ founder, *has utilized every media to communicate* the supernatural good news of Jesus Christ and the power of the Holy Spirit to a lost and dying world." (Emphasis added)

Tragically, they're not kidding! I wonder how many of his supporters know exactly what kind of media he was using when he was exposed or if he is still using it today.

Frankly, people who do these kinds of things in the name of God make many people (including me) sick to their stomachs. How can someone use their calling (if they really have one, that is) in this way and get away with it? Good question! The truly tragic thing is that phonies muddy the water and create doubt in things that truly are of God. The public sees such fakery and many conclude that any kind of supposed supernatural or divine intervention must not be real. This baloney steers many people away from the faith or at least posits them in such a skeptical position they can no longer find it in themselves to believe in anything supernatural. What a crime!

Of all the places that fakes, thieves, and impostors should not victimize others, it should be the church. However, though the level of technology is far beyond that of Bible times, false teachers and false prophets are nothing new. The writers of the New Testament dealt with them constantly.

One example is from an early church leader—the apostle Paul. In preparing the elders of the church for his departure from them, he warned them by saying,

> "I know that after I leave, savage wolves will come in *among you* and will not spare the flock. *Even from your own number* men will arise and distort the truth in order to draw away disciples after them. So be on your guard!"[59] (Emphasis added)

Jesus himself warned his followers about them. His friend Matthew recorded the following statements from the lips of the savior in chapter 7 of his gospel:

> "Beware of false prophets who come disguised as harmless sheep but are really vicious wolves. You can identify them by their fruit, that is, by the way they act. Can you pick grapes from thornbushes, or figs from thistles? A good tree produces good fruit, and a bad tree produces bad fruit. A good tree can't produce bad fruit, and a bad tree can't produce good fruit. So every tree that does not produce good fruit is chopped down and thrown into the fire. Yes, just as you can identify a tree by its fruit, so you can identify people by their actions. Not everyone who calls out to Me, 'Lord! Lord!' will enter the Kingdom of Heaven. Only those who actually do the will of My Father in heaven will enter. On judgment day many will say to Me, 'Lord! Lord! We prophesied in Your name and cast out demons in Your name and performed many miracles in Your name.' But I will reply, 'I never knew you. Get away from Me, you who break God's laws.'"[60]

Many who witness these swindlers would echo Jesus' words above. "Get away from me, you who break God's laws!" If the Son of God feels that way, why wouldn't any other sincere truth seeker?

DOES GOD HAVE MULTIPLE PERSONALITIES? (DENOMINATIONS)

Sybil. If you grew up in the '60s or '70s, that name reminds you of a movie starring actress Sally Field. The movie was based on a true story about a young lady whose childhood was so traumatic, that she eventually developed thirteen different personalities to deal with her pain.[61] Can you imagine? Some readers may be too young to remember that, but most of my generation could hardly forget it. As Sybil tried to deal with the pain of her past with her counselor, there were continual flashbacks in her memory of hurtful events. Each time that happened in her therapy sessions, a different personality would emerge. Her facial expression and even her voice would change as this new "person" responded to the therapist's comments or questions. The analyst would then try to unravel the theme of what each personality would express and attempt to trace it back to the original incident that sparked its creation. What a maze to try to grasp and apply! Do you see any parallels as you look at the church world? Have you ever asked yourself why the church of Jesus Christ seems to have so many personalities?

It is my understanding that there are over two hundred denominations that fall under the banner of Christendom. Yet each one seems to feel that what they believe is the truth. When our family and some friends started a new church from scratch, as part of getting the word out, we sent ten thousand postcards advertising some meetings and inviting people to consider coming with us to start a new church. In the midst of that, I received an e-mail from a woman of a different denomination. She told me plainly that God only has one church, and her denomination is the only true one that Jesus founded!

As I stated earlier, I was raised Roman Catholic. In fact, I didn't even meet my first Protestant till I was twelve years old. (I kept looking for the pitchfork and devilish horns on his head. I was amazed that he looked so normal!) I really did not know much about other denominations because in the town of my boyhood years, one was hard-pressed to find anyone who was not Roman Catholic.

As a young adult, I remember hearing about the Baptist church, and then after discussion with one who attended such a church came to realize that there were a variety of that denomination's churches. There is the American Baptist, Independent Baptist, Southern Baptist, and more. As far as I knew, there was only one

Catholic church (though I have since discovered there are even a couple strains of that denomination) so this was confusing to me.

Now I do not mean to pick on the Baptist denomination as by this stage of life, I am aware that many denominations have several strains. The Lutheran church has the Evangelical Lutheran Church in America, as well as the Lutheran Church-Missouri Synod[62] and even the Wisconsin Synod.[63] The Christian church denomination has one strain known as The Disciples of Christ. The fellowship called the Church of Christ also has the United Church of Christ. Though not truly affiliated with the official Church of Christ, a leader of the Boston Church of Christ told me his church and those of that connection are the only true church. The Methodist movement has the Evangelical and the United sects. The Church of God has the Church of God in Christ, the Church of God in Prophecy, as well as the Church of God, Cleveland, Tennessee.

To add to the variety, each church of each branch of each denomination (of which I have only mentioned a few) has their own personality. I remember one Easter Sunday when my family and I went to visit a church in Maine that was of the same denomination I am affiliated with. I had only been a part of one Bible-teaching church in my home state of Rhode Island since my conversion, and thus, I had only seen our church's personality. That church in Maine, though the same denomination with all the same basic beliefs was so incredibly different than my home church, if I had not seen the sign on the marquee, I would never have even guessed there was any connection! From the music style to the average age of the parishioners to the décor of the sanctuary and even the speaking style of the minister, it was nothing...*nothing* like what I was used to. I was amazed.

I recall during my tenure as a youth minister that several of the churches in the area (Catholic and Protestant) were trying to get our congregations together in a show of unity to the public. Many arguments and tensions followed and, if my memory serves me correctly, the event never even took place because of that.

Some of the leaders even seemed to become antagonist toward one another. All this from a religion that professes to represent the God of love who gave His only Son to die on a cross where He prayed for His murderers, "*Father, forgive them, for they do not know what they are doing.*"[64] (emphasis added)

Each denomination and church believes that at least some, if not all or most, of their foundation is based on the Bible and on the words of Jesus. Yet from the gospel of John we read that on the night of his arrest, Jesus prayed to the Father for His followers and asked that

> [21] all of them may be one, Father, just as You are in Me and I am in You...*so that the world may believe that You have sent Me*...that they may be one as We are one: I in them and You in Me. May they be brought to *complete unity to let the world know that You sent Me.*"[65] (emphasis added.)

Could the lack of complete unity in the church be the very reason that so many do not believe that the Father really sent Jesus?

Further, in a letter to the believers in the city of Ephesians, Paul the Apostle spoke of the church of Jesus Christ by saying, "There is one body [of believers]"[66] To the average human mind, this is a big dilemma. Many would ask, "Which body is *the* 'one' or do they altogether make up the 'one body?' If so, why do they seem to disagree so much if their beliefs are based on the same supposedly inspired book?" These are not small questions in the minds of the unconvinced!

As a young adult, when I began searching for God more intensely than I ever had, I remember feeling confused by the whole denomination aura. As I began to read the Bible, questions naturally arose. I reasoned that every minister or leader of any church I would go to in order to ask questions would simply give me his or her denominational view. How could anyone, especially someone like me who was anything but religious, have even the slightest clue of which one would be right? I do not think I am alone in that feeling of bewilderment. I believe that even today, as the seekers of truth formulate their inquiries, they look at all of God's personalities in the different denominations and feel that Christians seem even more confused than they are! To many postmodern minds, this is an enormous roadblock in the path of pursuing spiritual reality.

CLOSING COMMENTS
ON THIS CHAPTER

I want to close this chapter with some comments and observations. The truth is not always pretty, yet it is always necessary. This chapter has been the longest in this book thus far. My intention has simply been to confess that there are legitimate problems in the church world that contradict what Bible-believing Christians proclaim and even what the book itself asserts. When those outside of the church world look at her representatives and consider the God they advocate, they see a serious gulf between our confessions and our conduct. The reason is often because it is real. As they say, it is what it is. No need to candycoat, minimize, or excuse it. This chapter has been a somewhat raw look at that reality.

In discussing these things, as a Christ followers, I have indicted myself, as well as those with whom I am spiritually related. This is an intentional vulnerability. You may wonder, why would a writer present such arguments that convict him and the very cause for which he lives? First of all, it is because I believe that the truth is essential whether it's pleasant or not. In the Gospel of John, Jesus made the following statement: "Then you will know the truth, and the truth will set you free."[67] Notice that it is not *the truth* in and of itself that *will set you free*. Truth exists now; it existed long before Jesus came to earth and has continued to exist long after He went back to heaven, yet many people are not truly free. This fact is revolutionary when one really lets it sink in. It is when we *know the truth* that it finally provides the power for us to be *set free.* So in order for us to be free *from* being held captive by these flaws in the church and free *to* experience what God intended for His people, we must *know* (i.e., recognize, acknowledge, and accept) *the truth.* Glossing over these matters with nice religious platitudes and pat answers will only keep us chained to it. That's why this book is purposely transparent.

Secondly, and most importantly, I want to ask whoever reads this book to do the same thing—become vulnerable and open enough to face the truth, whether the reader feels pleasant about what they discover or not. Whether it challenges one's cherished beliefs, upbringing, or generational traditions, or whether it does none of that, I encourage you to face the music. In *knowing* the truth in the *present,* you will have the power to receive freedom from the *past* and be far more likely to have a quality *future.* Sounds good to me. How about you?

Before you read the next chapter, whether you have surrendered to Him or not, please ask God to show you the truth and help you be vulnerable enough to face it in a healthy way. Don't know how to pray? Just talk to God from your heart as you would to a caring loving parent or grandparent. You do not need any special words. He is not impressed by long, loud, or lengthy prayers. Words of sixteenth-century Shakespearian English do not capture His attention any more than common, everyday language. The heart of God is touched by an honest soul sincerely searching to understand Him and His ways with the genuine intent to follow them (that's the real key). In fact, Jeremiah, who was a prophet, quoted God as saying, "You will seek Me and find Me when you seek Me with *all* your heart."[68] He also said, "Call to Me and *I will answer you* [emphasis added] and tell you great and unsearchable things you do not know."[69]

So just ask Him to help you. Yes, it is really that simple!

Okay, let's now consider some other things in response to all those apparent contradictions.

5

THE COUNTERACTION

THE RESPONSE TO THE CONTRADICTIONS

As a pastor, I have had the privilege and duty of advising many people over the years. From young children to seniors and every age in the middle, I have heard what seems to me to be an innumerable amount of human issues. However, I have spent the most time counseling couples. King Solomon once wrote that "the first to present his case seems right."[70] I have found that to be so true. After decades of pastoral counseling, I am keenly aware that there are two sides to every story. The rest of that Proverb says, "Till another comes forward and questions him." This chapter is a section-by-section response to the previous chapter. The aim of this chapter is to come "forward and question [i.e., respond to]" those issues with the same candor and vulnerability as they were first asserted.

UNLIMITED POWER

Most of us have probably never heard of Wapakoneta, Ohio. It is a small town south of Fort Wayne, Indiana. Its population in 2007 was just over 9400 people.[71] In 1930, it was far less than that. Yet in that little town in that rather obscure year of history, a baby boy was born who would put that little town on the proverbial map about forty years later.

July 20, 1969, is an important day, not only in American history but for the entire human race. On that day, at 4:17 p.m. Eastern Standard Time, mankind accomplished "its single greatest technological achievement of all time."[72] I still remember the now famous words uttered from mission commander Neil Armstrong of the Apollo 11 space team the moment he became the first man on the moon. "One small step for man, one giant leap for mankind." I recognize that there have been many space shuttles since then, to the moon and beyond. However, in 1969, that was an *astounding* accomplishment.

I have watched several space shuttle liftoffs, and I am always amazed at what appears to be an astronomical amount of power expended to launch the tonnage of that craft off the earth and into outer space. The total power of a space shuttle at the time of takeoff is about 12 billion watts of power or 16 million horsepower![73] Just to bring a little perspective, understand that one horsepower is equal to 745.699872 watts of power![74] As they say, you do the math. The engines work together to produce over 7 million pounds of thrust.[75] The amount of energy and power needed to propel such a vessel into space staggers the imagination. Yet it hardly amounts to child's sparkler in comparison to the power of Almighty God. I do not know this because I read it in a book or heard it from someone else. I know it because I, along with a multitude of others, have experienced it firsthand.

As I have discussed earlier, my religious experience prior to 1981 was noticeably void of any genuine power encounter. I believed growing up and into my young adult years that a supreme being existed and held omnipotent power somehow. Thus I do not mean I was unaware that such *good* power existed nor was I in any true sense an atheist. I had just never experienced it myself nor could I have ever dreamed of the incredible depth and purity of it; thus, it had no impact on me. Frankly, any religious person I encountered who did anything more than just show up at the church building to fulfill their obligation always struck me as kooky. Little did I know they had what I had been searching for all my life and for which I almost lost my soul in its pursuit.

I can still recall my first genuine encounter with the power and presence of God. In the early days of my newfound relationship with Him, my parents were a bit concerned about me. After all, watching your son walk out of the house with a Bible under his arm who used to walk out with a couple of six packs was a little difficult for them to grasp. Frankly, I hardly knew what to make of it myself.

Their desire was to keep me in the denomination that they raised me in and that all of our family was attached to. So when I began to pursue spiritual things, they naturally wanted me to talk to their priest and to attend meetings at their church. I was just twenty-one years old when I went with my parents to attend a meeting with people touched by what they called the Charismatic Renewal. This was a time where God seemed to be lovingly interrupting people's typical religious life and causing a new excitement and fervor about their relationship with Him than most had experienced. They were being filled with the Holy Spirit. This was more than people just getting more religious minded; it was an inner revolution of the heart away from selfishness toward God. Their entire demeanor and approach to life was immensely different than any religious or spiritual people I had known.

When we entered that room in another building of our parish, I could see immediately that these people were *very* different in a good way. They seemed far more genuine and sincere than the regular people in our church. They greeted each other with smiling embraces while looking each other right in the eye and greeting one another as *brother* or *sister*. I was mesmerized from the moment I entered. The people kindly greeted us as well, and I could tell they were truly happy we had come! In a congregation of two thousand people, I had never felt what this small group of twenty to twenty-five people simply exuded. Not that I would know, but it felt like being around Jesus.

They started with a prayer but not the recited (nearly mindless) memorized kind I had always heard. The man spoke from his heart with great reverence, but at the same time, it was like he was talking to a very close friend, someone he knew well. That alone was radical to me.

One man who drove an 18-wheeler stood up and told a story of God's protection in some odd circumstances. He had been held up several minutes with some malfunction of his truck he could not seem to figure out. After tinkering with it awhile, he got the truck going and headed down the highway very frustrated. As he did, he came upon the scene of an accident where the rear axle from another truck had somehow severed from it and bounced down the highway. He realized he would have been right behind that vehicle if his truck had not malfunctioned. He saw the hand of God in that. When he finished, they all verbalized their gratitude to God. I was fascinated by the whole thing.

Then a man stood up with his guitar and encouraged us to stand as he led us in a couple of worship songs. Though there was not much flair or pizzazz to it—no drums, electric guitars, or quality sound system—I again sensed a sincerity I had never seen. Yet it was more than that. There was the sense of a presence I had never known. Someone else was in that room that we could not see and the warm power with which He seemed to embrace us all was hard to put into words. Then it happened.

As the music and singing died down to a quiet tone, someone began to speak out in a language I had never heard. When he did, everyone in the room instantly grew silent and listened attentively. The moment he finished, someone else gave a beautiful message of God's love and concern, which seemed to be an interpretation of what the first person had said. Again, the rest of this group of God seekers responded with quiet words of adoration to God for "speaking" to them. It seemed like a gentle breeze just blew through that little ordinary room. Even these decades later, I can still recall turning to my mother who was sitting next to me and asking in a hushed but exuberant tone, "What was *that*?" Yet somehow I *knew* it was God. This was so much more exciting than anything I had experienced inside or outside the church world! I could sense that His power was so immense and unlimited that He could crush anyone of us or all of us, if He so desired. At the same time, I could also sense a gentle and genuine love diffusing like a fragrance of deep concern. This was a power I had never known even *existed* in the real world in any life-influencing way.

Two things so plain to me in such gatherings was (and, may I add, still are) the authentic sincerity of the people gathered and the sense of that powerful yet gentle presence I had encountered early on in my search for God and truth. These people were not cold, religious practitioners steeped in empty, lifeless traditions that do not impact one's daily life. Hardly!

My religious background had conditioned me to think that religious services consisted of a regimented programmed gathering that was almost entirely the same each and every time; one could hardly sneeze if it was not a programmed part of the ritual! We were like spectators watching a performance of professionals go through the order of the ceremony. The very idea that God himself might interrupt the plan would seem totally outlandish and out of order, to say the least. That all changed in my life in the early 1980s when I started attending a Bible-teaching, Spirit-filled church. The same powerful, yet gentle and sweet presence I felt in that charismatic renewal meeting was obvious there as well. It did not matter what denominational title one bore; these people and the power present in these times together were the *real McCoy*!

Little did I know when that happened in 1981 that that experience of God's power was only a snippet of what I would encounter over the years. Just a few months after that, I had an experience that I have never forgotten, though decades have passed. It was so amazing and powerful yet so incredibly out of the box, I hardly told a soul for years.[76]

> My friend's mother and his brother led me to Christ and it was clear to me that they had experienced God in a way I had never known. They warned me that, once a person receives Christ, they enter into a very real spiritual war. His mother even showed me a cross that was literally ripped from her neck and broken into pieces while they visited an area known for its involvement in voodoo. They further explained to me that I could expect some kind of attempt by the devil to lure or scare me back into my old life. With some of the experiences that I had had before coming to Christ, this newfound information truly frightened me.
>
> Shortly thereafter, I was asked to stay at my sister's house and care for their family dog while they went away on vacation. They had a beautiful, large two-story cape not far from the Atlantic Ocean. I figured that if the enemy was going to do anything, it would probably be during my time there. I was correct in that assumption.
>
> Since many years have passed, some of the details of my daily schedule are a little sketchy. However, as I recall, I was working during the day and attending classes at a state junior college. On this particular night, I was studying at the kitchen table in my sister's home. My fear of what

the enemy might do combined with my lack of spiritual knowledge produced in me great anxiety as I studied.

Suddenly, I had a sense of terror so intense that I was afraid to even lift my gaze from my studies, convinced I would see a demon if I did. I know of no other way to describe it, then an overwhelming fear and sense that I was in the presence of something or someone I did not care to be!

I got on the phone and called my friend's mother to ask her to pray for me. She was busy, so I told him the situation and asked him to mention it to her so she would pray for me. As a new believer, I felt certain she had far more influence with God than I did. Still consumed with fear, I went back to my studies.

All of a sudden, a peace washed over me like I had never known or even heard of, and every trace of fear evaporated. It was instantaneous and the contrast between the way I felt just moments before and the peace that consumed me was positively amazing! There wasn't even one hint of fear in me!

Not understanding such things in any size, shape, or form and realizing my newfound spiritual walk had to have something to do with it, I simply lifted my gaze toward heaven and said, "I don't know what this is, but thank you, Lord!" I saw that the clock read 9:45 and I made a mental note of it. I basked in this experience for a little while, and still filled with awe, I then went back to my studies, rejoicing in the Lord.

When I was done studying, I made sure my sister's dog went outside and then came back in for the night. I then went to go upstairs to bed, and I will never forget what happened. As I walked through the dining room, I began to feel a heavenly presence, which became more and more pronounced as I climbed the stairs to the bedroom. By the time I reached the room, the presence was so intense that I honestly thought I was going to see Jesus! With all the partying I had done in the years before, I had experienced all kinds of earthly "highs." But this experience was so far beyond that and so much better; it would be like comparing heaven to hell. The peace and the security were such that I felt if Satan himself were in front of me, I would literally spit in his eye and laugh!

As I climbed in bed, I am sure my eyes were as big as half dollars as I strained forward fully, expecting Jesus to appear. I had no idea what this was or what it meant, but I sat in the bed, weeping in a deep sense of gratitude to God. Surely, this experience was from Him, and I could not believe that the God of all the galaxies cared enough to touch such a wretched sinner as me in this way! I thanked Him over and over again through my tears of immeasurable joy and wonder.

I do not know how long I sat there, but I eventually fell asleep. It was the best sleep I have ever experienced in my entire life. When I awoke, I literally felt as if I had been born all over again. Every sin I had committed in the past seemed to have been washed away, and I felt brand-new. Even my body felt totally refreshed with no sense of discomfort or grogginess. This all felt so very amazing to me, but little did I know that there was more to come!

After I went through that next day's routine of work and classes, I called my friend's mother that evening. I asked her if her son had spoken to her about my fear the night before and wondered if she had prayed for me. She affirmed that she did, and still curious about what had actually happened to me, I asked what she prayed and when. She said she prayed that God would *surround my bed with a legion of His angels and that He would allow me to feel their presence!* A legion is between 3000 and 6000! I do not know if there were that specific amount, but I almost fell over when I realized what had happened! These eternal, mighty beings resonated with the presence of the Almighty One who had commissioned them to stand sentinel over me! I then asked her about what time she prayed, and she said that it was 9:45. I could hardly believe all this, but it was clearly true!

Over twenty years have come and gone since that incredible night, but I have never forgotten the wonder and awe of that experience.[77]

Though none have equaled the intensity of that particular incident, I witnessed many more expressions of God's power through the years. Some of them were outside of the walls of any religious building and some were not. Let me tell you more.

I started smoking when I was twelve years old. Like many kids in my era, I was just experimenting. The first several times I stole a cigarette from my mother's pack, snuck up into my tree fort, and coughed my lungs out in my attempt to be cool. Sadly, smoking cigarettes eventually became a life-controlling habit. Typically I would go through about a pack and a half in a day. If I was drinking and partying, it was about double that. Over the years, I became so addicted to nicotine that I could not—please understand—*could not* endure more than four hours without a cigarette unless I was sleeping. No joke. I would get so dizzy I felt like I was high and could hardly function.

When I became a follower of Christ in 1981, it was not long before a desire to quit became very strong in me. I did not see it as a rule I had to keep to impress God or one of those "thou shalt not" things. I really just felt like God had better things for me than doing something that was hurting my body which was now His temple.[78] So out of love and reverence for my Savior, I determined I would quit.

For roughly the next eighteen months, I tried every conceivable approach I could think of. Some readers will recall the filters that were popular, which a smoker could put their cigarette in. The filters were meant to slowly wean a person off the nicotine. All it did for me was make me smoke more to get my nicotine fix. I tried cutting down until I was just smoking a few a day, but the time in between was unbearable. The level of mental and emotional pressure, as well as the physical addiction, can only be understood by one who has been through such a battle. It is truly a prison, at least it certainly was for me. After nearly ten years of addiction, there just seemed to be no way out. Even praying did not seem to help. Well, God had a plan in mind.

I talked with some fellow believers who really believed in the power of prayer. As we talked and considered the promises of the Bible, I was encouraged and inspired. I actually set a date to quit. Because I was attending a trade school at the time, I had to plan around classes or that dizziness would make it hard to sit in class. I told some friends from my Christian singles group my plan, and they committed to praying for me to quit on that particular day. Though I was encouraged, I kept vacillating between hope and despair as nothing seemed to make any difference. Frankly, I was so weary from the battle, I told God that this would be my last attempt to quit. That unless He would take away the actual desire and need completely, I would surrender to the fact that I would be a believer who would smoke the rest of my life.

What happened on what was to be my last day of smoking is etched in my mind forever. I was a machinist at the time and was sitting at my bench and operating a spindle drill. I was simply talking softly to the Lord while I worked and telling Him my desperate need for Him to completely remove this battle from my life and take away my very desire to smoke. Suddenly, I heard a voice in my heart. It was not an audible sound but just as clear in my spirit. The Lord said, "Your victory has already been won; just receive it." It was so clear I turned around to see if anyone around me heard it, but of course, they did not. I was inspired beyond words! I did not have to try to muster up faith to believe what I was just told. There was no more human effort required. I do not know why this did not happen the other times I prayed, but it certainly did *this* time! There is such an immense difference between *believing* something will be and *knowing* it will. I did not just believe. I *knew* God would come through, and come through He did!

That night, I went to my classes at trade school, finished my cigarettes, and threw the pack away. When I woke up the next day, the desire was totally gone without any withdrawals or physical discomforts of any kind! One could not even tempt me with a cigarette. I had absolutely no desire whatsoever to have one! It has been said that when one comes to the end of themselves, they come to the beginning of God. Well, that is what happened to me. I have never returned to that habit. God's amazing power was demonstrated in my life that day. It was not my willpower; I did not have any. It was nothing...nothing...I did. It was the power of God. No theological or philosophical debate could ever convince me otherwise. The God who gave His only Son had stepped into my struggle and set me free!

Let me share another personal story by first stating that I was terrified of public speaking. In fact, I was so afraid of it that I resigned as class president in high school during my junior year out of fear that I would have to speak at graduation the following year. There was no way I was going to stand up in front of hundreds of people and talk into a microphone!

About six months after I surrendered the control of my life to the Lord Jesus Christ, I somehow knew in my heart that I would be in full-time vocational ministry one day. Of course, that would eventually lead to public speaking. God would need to come to my aid again and in a big way.

After my conversion, I became more involved in my local church, and soon the leadership recognized the call on my life that I was already aware of in my heart. Our pastor decided to mentor some younger men in the church who felt a call to ministry. He chose twelve of which I was one.

Over the next year, he began to meet with us and try to coach us along. He also determined he would schedule each man in a rotation to lead in different ways during the services (e.g., lead in prayer, receive the offering, etc.) I politely thanked him but flat refused because that would mean getting up in front of people and speaking into a mic. Not me! No way, no how! Thankfully, he was gracious to me and allowed me to continue under his tutelage without having to speak publicly for about a year.

Let me again illustrate the depth of my fear of public speaking. Frankly, it was more like *terror*. My pastor used to end the services by randomly asking someone in the congregation to stand and close in a prayer. When he would get to that part of the service, I would literally duck my head down and hide behind the people sitting in front of me. If I even *thought* he was going to pick on me, I started to gag and felt like I was going to vomit!

Our pastor took the twelve of us to a pastor's school at a megachurch in New Orleans in 1984. During the time we were there, I spoke to God about this whole thing in prayer. I said something like, "Lord, if you have really called me to be a minister, this has got to stop. Eventually, I am going to *have* to stand up and speak in front of people. I am going to tell the pastor to give me a date to speak and, frankly Lord, I'd rather vomit in front of the whole church and know that I am not really called than to continue in this state of limbo!"

Well, the pastor and I settled on a date for me to speak. I spent many hours preparing a sermon. Besides the congregation, my parents and some relatives came to hear me. If I was going to bomb, at least there would be plenty of witnesses! All that day at my regular job, I quietly talked to the Lord about what lay ahead that evening and how I really needed His help.

If you were around then, do you remember where you were when Neil Armstrong landed on the moon? (No, this is not a misplaced paragraph. Please read on.) Do you remember where you were when President Ronald Regan was shot? How about where you were when you heard the news about Princess Diana, Mother Teresa, Michael Jackson, Kurt Cobain, or Whitney Houston? September 11? Some things in life make such an indelible mark on your mind you can recall the exact spot you were when they occurred no matter how many years pass. Well,

I could take you to the very spot where this power encounter with the Lord took place. I will never forget what happened that Wednesday night in 1984.

*   *   *

When I followed the pastor out to ascend the steps to the platform, something happened to me that changed me forever. As I put my foot on that first step, a peace literally washed over me from my head to my feet, and every trace of fear completely vanished in a moment. It did not simply fade slowly so that I suddenly realized it was gone. It lifted in an instant. I was concerned and troubled one moment and totally fearless the next. When I came to the pulpit to share my message, I was no more nervous than I am writing right now as I sit alone at my computer screen typing these words. Since that moment, I have never been the slightest bit nervous to speak publicly. Over these twenty-five-plus years of ministry, I have spoken to many people—groups as small as a few people to crowd of hundreds, and I have never experienced fear or nervousness again. Not one time.

May I pose the obvious question? If that was not God, how would you explain what happened? While a person may experience a moment of euphoria after an extreme inner struggle and their sense of surrender to their issue, surely it would not last over twenty-five years. Even if their nervousness somehow magically disappeared, that still would not of itself make them an effective speaker so that hundreds of people would gather to hear them share their insights for over two decades, would it? Not likely. In fact, let's talk straight. There is no way that would happen. No, friend, that was the supernatural, life-changing power of the living God described in the pages of the Bible. Period.

Time and space do not allow me to share every encounter I have had or know of between then and now. However, let me share with you a more recent *power encounter* with the God of the Bible.

One Sunday during a worship service, I was grooving with the music (yes, you can do that in church), singing out my adoration of God, and lifting my hands in worship. The tune we were singing contained a line in the chorus to the effect of "Oh Jesus, where would I be without You?" We sang that several times, and frankly, my mind had begun to shift to autopilot. You know, when we begin to get so used to something we start to do it, but our hearts are beginning to disengage.

That was my state of mind as I sang that line one more time. Well, all of sudden, without any warning, sensation, or fanfare, a mental image literally took over my mind. I saw myself sitting in a prison yard with a bandana around my head, my arms covered in tattoos, and a cigar in my mouth as I sat around playing cards with some other inmates! To say the least, I was startled to the core. The Lord had answered my question.

Somehow, some way, *that* would have been my destiny had the Lord not arrested my heart in 1981. This revelation was a divine act of God's Spirit and demonstrated His amazing power. It also communicates the power of God to redirect a person's entire destiny if we allow Him to.

Surely, not everyone who reads this book is headed for something that negative without Jesus in their life. But this I know for certain. His power in the life of those who truly surrender to Him will bring about a far better, more fulfilling life than you could ever assemble in your own ingenuity, talents, and skills, not to mention in the *hereafter*!

Many complain about the powerlessness of the church these days in light of what the scriptures say compared with what we see. While I concur that there seems to be some kind of hindrance, a church of Bible-believing, faithful, Spirit-filled believers is still the most powerful place on earth. The miracles in my life did not occur in the parties, bars, and nightclubs I frequented. While education is a great thing, the power I experienced did not occur in any classroom or hall of philosophical conjecture. As much fun as being in friend's and family member's homes has been, those power encounters did not occur there either. No, they took place where Christ followers prayed and simply trusted in the words from the God of the Bible. Where His people gather, be it in a temple, church building, Starbucks, or bowling alley, they ARE the church. That is where true, life-changing, destiny-altering, character-shaping power resides like no where else in all of creation!

I could fill volumes with stories of the power of God I have witnessed over the years. I have only mentioned my own conversion. However, let me say that the God of the Bible so completely changed my heart and life on September 6, 1981, that I became a whole new person. The person I was does not even exist anymore.[79]

In my teenage years, I was into everything from vandalism to arson, from premarital sex and pornography to robbery, from credit card fraud to drugs, and on and on the list goes. Yet when Jesus Christ came into my life, every desire and goal of my life changed. It was not that I had to *make* myself be a more moral or better person; I knew that I was totally incapable of that in my own power. No, the power of God radically changed every single thing about the way I thought, what was important to me, as well as my likes and dislikes to the point that I can hardly imagine that I was the person I used to be. Please understand that I am not claiming that I am now sinless, somehow holier-than-thou or better than others. I have come to know in the deepest part of me that I am no better than *any* other person on this planet, no matter his lifestyle, status, or lack thereof. No, the only reason I have been changed is the grace of a God who loves sinners so deeply that He gave His only Son to rescue us from the power, pain, and penalty that always eventually comes with a life without Him—a life of sin.

The power of God is prevalent where people believe on Him from their hearts and take the promises of His word seriously. Why in just one trip to an impoverished part of Mexico that I was part of in 1993 with about fifty young people, we saw eighteen confirmed miracles. I have heard prophetic words spoken from people to others in need who knew nothing of their situation in advance, and there was no explanation but God. I have seen many people healed of cancer and a variety of other illnesses, watched addicts of every kind be set free and changed. Truly, the list is almost endless. That is no exaggeration. That is not hype to sell this book you hold. It is reality.

Oh, I am well aware that the church is not a perfect place, but isn't that because it is made up of imperfect people? Aside from the flaws (that every other organization has as well) where else could a person go to receive such incredible demonstrations of the power and love of God? Only the church!

UNDYING LOVE

After my experiences in the church world, I did not equate going there with acceptance or love. It was quite the opposite. When I came to faith in Christ in 1981, going to church was not really high on my priority list. Like many, I felt that if I just faithfully read the Bible and prayed I could know and love God without having to show up at a particular building once a week. Also, over the years, what I had witnessed at religious gatherings told me that the majority of churchgoers looked and carried themselves a certain way. Everything from the length of their hair to the style of their clothing, once thing was for sure: I would not fit in.

I had shoulder-length hair, some tattoos, I rode a motorcycle, wore a leather jacket, jeans, sneakers, T-shirts, and smoked like a chimney. From my perspective, I would be like a fish out of water in any church. However, after some months in the Bible and prayer, I decided that I should check it out.

To be candid, I went there with a bit of a chip on my shoulder, half-expecting that the people would look down on me or avoid me. I expected to be rejected at some level. I must say, I was pleasantly surprised when I found the exact opposite, just as I did in that first small group attended at my parish I mentioned in a previous chapter. I had never felt so accepted and welcomed anywhere as I did there. I can say without any hint of reservation, they embraced me and were more than willing to receive me as one of their own. I never felt judged, frowned upon, or ostracized in the slightest bit. For the first time in my life, I felt genuinely loved in a gathering of churchgoers! Because *they* accepted me, it made it much easier to believe, accept, and experience the love of the One who filled them with the love they so clearly exuded—Jesus. It was awesome!

I can still vividly recall attending my first single adult gathering at the leader's home. These churchgoers seemed to have a set of code words I eventually came to understand the meaning of. They called this get-together a *fellowship*. Believe it or not, but I had never heard that word before.

I did not even know how to dress, so I donned myself in what I thought were church clothes (a three-piece suit) and headed to the meeting. I just wanted to fit in, you know, blend in with these *religious* people. My usual attire sort of matched my long hair and tattooed arms—jeans, T-shirt, and sneakers. I then walked into what turned out to be nothing more than a summer cookout and party without booze, pot, or drugs. I was a little nervous because I still felt a little out of place, especially since I smoked. I thought these *holy* people would surely see me as a round peg trying to fit in a square hole. Once again, I found the opposite.

Well, I must admit that when I stepped foot in the house and saw everyone in jeans and casual clothes, I felt a little foolish. When I went outside for a smoke later on, I was all apologies. Not a word of condemnation from anyone. No unsolicited advice. No Bible verses quoted at me to make me feel worse than I already did. Nothing but the things I was learning were business as usual for these people—love and acceptance. This was a whole new experience for me. I would later realize that I would experience such things repeatedly for the next twelve-plus years that I attended there.

It is important to mention that, prior to my experiences with these Bible-believing, Spirit-filled Christians, it was rare for people's acceptance and love to not have some kind of price tag attached. Drinking buddies accepted me as long as I drank, but when I tried to stop and was trying to learn how to follow Jesus, I discovered it was not really *me* they cared about. It was actually how I made them laugh when I was acting like them that they loved. As soon as that changed, they did not appreciate my presence. The love of girlfriends was secure as long as I was doing the things they wanted. Again, it wasn't *me* they cared about but how I made them feel at the time when I was cooperating with their wishes for me. From school teachers to coaches, bosses, and even some of my own family members when I was no longer their religious *flavor*, it became clear that their love was conditional to one degree or another. Not so with these new believers I connected with. Oh, they had flaws just like me, but their love was not typically conditional and withdrawn when I did not line up. The love they so beautifully lived out came from the One who had loved them (and all of us) so perfectly—Jesus.

In 1984–1985, I went through a very difficult time. I was twenty-five years old, single, and lonely. Also, my job was far less than pleasant with two men in authority over me who thrived on antagonizing me daily. Those things combined with a relationship that just was not right for me and an engagement I felt compelled to break off led to a serious depression that I could not seem to escape. It was a long time, and I felt far from God, empty inside, lacking direction and happiness.

Once again, my Christian friends were there to be supportive both through prayer, encouragement, and just about any way they could think of. One friend actually bought me a plane ticket to go visit another friend in Texas just to get me away from my situation and enjoy time together with caring people there. These people were amazing. They exemplified a love I had never seen. Although I had experienced it myself on a personal level from the Lord, I never had through people as I did in that first *renewal* meeting I mentioned earlier. These folks were the real deal. They walked with me until the depression lifted some eighteen months later.

*　　*　　*

Shortly after coming to faith, my father had a battle with congestive heart failure. He was just fifty-nine years old. Thankfully, he recovered from that bout; however, about six years later, his condition worsened till his heart doctor told us he had just a few months to live. That was a long, dark trek. His doctor was convinced that if we told my father his true condition that he would simply give up. Heeding the doctor's advice, we never told him. I still struggle to know if that was the right decision.

The next several months seemed like eternity as my dad went from bad to worse. He lost a lot of weight, had great difficulty sleeping, and was in and out of the hospital time and again. My job at the time put me less than a mile from home. I would come home every lunch time hoping that I would not find him having passed away. It was awful.

Saturday morning, November 7, 1987, with just he and I in the house, he had his final heart attack. I had just completed a CPR course, and to this day, my own father is the only person I have ever performed that technique on. That is a moment I will never forget. The pain of the whole monthlong experience was just awful. I remember when my mother and my siblings left the hospital broken up and exasperated, and there they were again, my Christian friends, literally waiting just outside the entrance. Supportive, encouraging, loving, and consoling. Even with all their flaws, they were so much like Jesus. It was just what I needed.

I will never forget what happened at my father's funeral arrangements. The church where I was the youth minister at the time had a Christian school. They shut down classes for the teenagers and brought them all to the wake (a.k.a. visitation). One by one, they lined up and passed by my father's casket and came to express their sympathies to me and my family. Those precious kids! The bond between us was supernatural. It was so out of the ordinary and noticeable that one of my aunts came up to me, overwhelmed with wonder and asked me, "What happened to you?" I knew exactly what she meant. There was no need to explain. She had known the selfish hellion I was before coming to faith in Christ. Now she was observing something so out of character for the person in me she once knew. She was overwhelmed. This was the love of Jesus—undying, unconditional, authentic. Something none of us deserve, and if anyone *did* deserve it, both she and I knew it certainly was not me.

Thus far, I have described the undying love of God as it has been expressed toward me from others. I could also share many more similar stories, as well as how that love became part of me. The love that was expressed *to* me over time began to flow *through* me as well. I had often felt so unacceptable and unloved in any genuine way except by a select few people. Over time, I came to realize the truth as stated by Dr. Neil Anderson, "The love of God is not dependent upon its object; it is dependent on His character."[80]

Earlier in this book, I was candid in sharing examples of professing believers who were not loving at all. Most people in our culture have had similar experiences from supposed religious people. However, even with all their shortcomings, my experience and that of many others suggests that the kind of undying supportive love available to each of us that is straight from God and through His people is unmatched anywhere else but in the church.[81]

I say this without a trace of condemnation or judgment. I learned that there is an enormous difference between *religious* people and those who have genuinely experienced the love and power of God. The term *Christian* is so watered down and bland in our culture it hardly carries any true meaning. In the book of Acts in the New Testament, chapter 11, we discover that *"The disciples were called Christians first at Antioch."*[82] (emphasis added) This new sect of people following the well-known prophet Jesus were so much like Him that they dubbed this new title to describe them—*Christian*, and it means "little Christ." It was not a compliment nor was it considered positive in even the remotest way. It was an antagonistic, sarcastic insult. The ancient historian Tactitus has been quoted as stating that "the vulgar call them Christians," and said they were "hated for their shameful acts" (i.e., defiance of the many gods others worshipped).[83]

Growing up I just assumed that everyone who went to church was a Christian. However, as has been said before, being in church makes you no more a Christian than sitting in McDonald's makes you a hamburger! The Bible does not define a Christian the way most of our culture does. Many simply think a Christian is someone who believes in God, is a nice person, and probably goes to church sometimes.

Concerning His true followers, Jesus said, "By this all men will know that you are My disciples, if you love one another"[84] Further, Jesus' friend John wrote in another letter, "We love because He first loved us. If anyone says, "I love God" yet hates his brother, *he is a liar*. For anyone who does not love his brother, whom he has seen, *cannot* love God, whom he has not seen. And He has given us this command: Whoever loves God must also love his brother"[85] (emphasis added). Many more verses could be quoted here with this general idea. However, the point is that love, true genuine love, is the hallmark of authentic Christians because it is the hallmark of the God they serve. John the Beloved further wrote, "God is love."[86] He does not just *give* or *inspire* love, He is love.

Friend, if you are looking for genuine undying, unconditional love, find a good Bible teaching church, and contrary to U2's lead singer Bono, you *will* find what you're looking for![87] If you show up and do *not* find that, pray for God to guide your steps and keep visiting Bible-teaching churches till you do. Sooner or later, He will lead you to where you fit, where His people display His true heart for you, and your search will be over. I do not share this from theory, from what I learned at college or graduate school nor from something I read in a book. Neither do I communicate it from hearing what others have said. I have come to know these truths from personal experience and from the testimonies of countless others. The love of God directly to believers and through His people is the most critical and necessary reality that every person needs. Most of us wander through life searching for what will finally satisfy our inner thirst, seldom realizing the very thing we are looking for to bring purpose to our lives was right in front of us the whole time. So God's Spirit and Jesus' bride (the church) say, "Come!"[88]

UNRIVALED RELEVANCE

Lucy was our family's beloved dog for sixteen years. A good-natured shepherd–miniature collie mix, she had a sweet disposition and never gave us a moment's trouble. She greeted all three of my sons with a good sniff and a wagging tail when we brought them home from the hospital where they were born. At the time we buried her, my boys were fifteen, thirteen, and eleven, and my wife and I had recently celebrated eighteen years of marriage. Lucy had been with us sixteen of those eighteen years. We have many memories of her, and they are all good. One thing I remember was the way she would tilt her head, focus her eyes, and lift her ears when there was a high-pitched sound or something she did not understand. You know that "tilt the head" look dogs give you as if to say, "What in the world was that?" Except for the lifting of the ears, most of us have similar responses (whether outwardly or inwardly) when something causes us confusion or we cannot connect it to any present reality.

Here is a perfect example. While enjoying a day off with my family recently, I received a text that said, "Asherah pole—steps—pursuit of happiness." I sat and stared at the little screen with that same confused tilt of the head that Lucy used to give. The text came from a troubled man in my church. I am sure the message meant something to him, but it bore no relevance to me. My religious experience years ago was similar to that until I attended the aforementioned church where the primary core value was a genuine belief in the Bible and its application to everyday life. There was a clear path from instruction to application, and the relevance of it all was evidenced in the lives of the people there.

Though we looked at this earlier, it seems important to recall the definition of relevance. *The American Heritage Dictionary* defines *relevance* as something that shows "pertinence to the matter at hand" or has "applicability to social issues."[89] When something is relevant, it means there is a clear connection between it and the need or issue at hand. In spiritual terms, it means that what is being asserted and even *how* it is being projected connects with the pertinent need, that there is an obvious way to apply it to one's situation or circumstances. In other words, there is a direct link between understanding the idea and how it fits in life. Though the church world may often use outdated *methods* to communicate to her listeners, many have discovered by first hand experience that the *messages* of biblical truth she declares could not be more relevant. I am consistently and constantly amazed at how the core of the issues that biblical characters faced hundreds and even thousands of years ago are not just *similar* but *identical* to the ones we face today. While the cultural application and settings may vary, the heart of the issues and the truths that apply do not.

Let's consider a few examples. The first one comes from approximately 6000 years ago. It appears in Genesis, the first book in the Bible.[90] There is one man that God sort of singled out. While this may seem like favoritism at first sight, nothing could be further from the truth. From this one man, God wanted to develop an entire nation to represent him well to the rest of the world. This man's name was Abram, and he is the progenitor of what we now know as the Jewish people.

In Genesis chapter 12, we are told about a famine so severe that Abram gathered up his family and left Canaan to travel south to Egypt. It was fairly well known that Egypt typically had a good supply of food primarily because it was situated near the Nile River. This great water source provided much of the nutrients needed for their cattle and crops to flourish. All of that made the food supply quite plentiful. So Abram made a wise practical decision to go there so his family could be fed and survive this difficult though temporary situation.

They didn't have trains, planes, or automobiles back then, so travel took a lot of time. Abram had lots of time to mull things over and consider what may happen once he got there. Have you ever seen someone enter a room and every head turn? Some people are just strikingly attractive. This was Abram's wife, Sarai. The Bible says she "was a very beautiful woman"[91] Keep in mind this was a different time and culture. Traveling with a beautiful woman could get a man in big trouble. The men in that area were likely to see a husband as the biggest barrier between their desires for the woman and actually fulfilling them. Actually, many men *still* feel that way deep inside. Our evil has just become a little more sophisticated with modern technology.

Abram began to think that his hot-looking wife may actually become a barrier to their (more accurately *his*) survival, the very reason they traveled all that way. So he developed a plan. In Genesis chapter 12, we see the conversation between Abram and Sarai.

"When the Egyptians see you, they will say, 'This is his wife.' Then they will kill me but will let you live. Say you are my sister, so that I will be treated well for your sake and my life will be spared because of you."

While this may appear as a total lie, it actually had truth to it. You see, they had the same father but not the same mother.[92] She was his half sister, but a *half*-truth is a *whole* lie.

Consider the issues that run like a thread through this account and ask yourself, do these things connect with our present day situations? Abram had to move his family to a place that was known to be a more prosperous area because their economic situation changed. He became fearful that things might go badly for him, so he asked his wife to lie for him. When the people he lied to found out, they became angry and told him to pick up his lying wife and leave. He repeated this same behavior in Genesis chapter 20 with the same results despite of this. Years later, his son Isaac followed his father's example and did the exact same thing to the son (or grandson) of the very man his father had done the exact same thing to! (See Genesis, chapter 26, verses 6–10.)

Do families sometimes move during hard economic times to regions their research shows them are more prosperous for the good of their family? Of course they do. Do men still ask their wives to lie for them because they are afraid of consequences in certain situations? Again, certainly. Do men with very attractive wives still struggle to trust other men around them? When people discover they have been lied to do they typically react with anger and expulsion in some way? Do children often repeat the behaviors of their parents even though they have witnessed the negative results? The answer to all these questions is the same— yes! Please keep in mind that this historical account is over 5000 years old, yet the issues and reactions of our present times do not really vary all that much, if at all.

Let's skip ahead a century or so to an incident between Abram's grandsons who were twin brothers. Believe it or not, their competitive power struggle began while they were still inside their mother![93] One brother, Esau, grew up to be a skillful hunter, while the other one liked staying at home and spending time with his mother.[94] Their father, Isaac, liked to eat wild game, so Esau the hunter became his favorite of the two sons. The mother (Rebekah) liked having Jacob home and, because she spent so much time with him, he became her favorite of the two sons.

Long story short, over the years, Jacob deceived his brother Esau a few times to gain notoriety and a greater inheritance. To make matters worse, their mother took sides, suggested a scheme to help Jacob deceive her other son and actually helped him do it![95] This favoritism caused an estrangement between these two brothers that lasted about twenty years and nearly led to a bloody battle before God intervened.[96]

Keeping in mind these situations occurred about the fifth millennia BC, ask yourself similar questions as the earlier example. Do brothers often become competitive and fight? Do parents sometimes develop a favorite child? Does that favoritism, real or perceived, often lead to an estrangement? Once again, the answer is the same—*absolutely*! Are there lessons that you and I can apply to our lives today? Of course! For one thing, parents are not wise to pick favorites among their children. If they do, they will cause problems among them that will more than likely still exist long after they are buried. Does this incident, recorded so many years ago, have anything relevant to say to the modern parenting world? Is it relevant? Clearly.

Solomon is said to have been the wisest man to have ever lived besides Jesus himself. Solomon, the son of King David of Israel, eventually replaced his father and became the most well-respected, wealthiest and wisest king of all the kings of the earth (around the tenth century BC). During his lifetime, he wrote well over 3000 proverbs so that others, particularly his sons, could benefit from his knowledge and wisdom. Surely, one might think that something written by someone who lived so long ago in a completely different time and culture would have nothing transcendent to say. Let's just consider a few of those proverbs to see if they pass the relevance test.

In Proverbs chapter 4, verse 23, Solomon wrote, "Above all else, guard your heart, for it is the wellspring of life." Is it not true that whatever is truly in the deepest part of a person comes out and overflows into every other part of his life and conduct? If a person "guards" what enters their mind and heart, do they not typically have a better quality outlook and life in general? Are these words any less true today than the day they were penned? Plainly, they are still applicable today.

In Proverbs chapter 6, verse 9, the king gives some advice concerning those who are lazy.

> How long will you lie there, you sluggard? When will you get up from your sleep? A little sleep, a little slumber, a little folding of the hands to rest—and poverty will come on you like a bandit and scarcity like an armed man.

Though it is not *always* the case, is not poverty often the result in the lives of those who refuse to work but would rather lounge around? Slothful people often seem surprised and overwhelmed when their vehicles are repossessed or their home is foreclosed on. Once again, do these words not have a direct application to our day and time?

A little further in the same chapter, Solomon tells us some of his many thoughts on adultery: "A man who commits adultery lacks judgment; whoever does so *destroys himself*. Blows and disgrace are his lot, and *his shame will never be wiped away.*" (emphasis added) When a man committed adultery, it was not a smart thing to do. The end results often ruined his life. In fact, by the Jewish laws, he was to be stoned to death so his evil ways would not spread through the community. Leviticus chapter 20, verse 10 reads, "If a man commits adultery with another man's wife—with the wife of his neighbor—both the adulterer and the adulteress must be put to death."

Even if he somehow got away with it or mercy was shown so he could continue to live, his shame would live on with him for all his life. From being shunned by the religious community, to facing the anger and potential violence from the woman's husband or family members to having his reputation ruined and respect lost, his life would never regain the strength it once had. While adultery is much more accepted today in America than it was then, isn't a great deal of this advice still sound today? Apart from being stoned to death, every other issue still follows people who commit adultery.

Okay, let's fast forward thousands of years closer to our day by looking at some of the things Jesus said. Again, let's consider if these words recorded two thousand years ago still connect with us in some relevant way. Matthew was one of Jesus' twelve closest friends. He recorded what has come to be known as the Sermon on the Mount from chapters five to seven of his book in the Bible. In chapter seven, Jesus taught, "In the same way you judge others, you will be judged, and with the measure you use, it will be measured to you." How different is this principle Jesus taught so long ago from the modern saying "what goes around comes around"? Truer words have never been spoken as far as I can see. Though there are always exceptions, generally speaking, people get back what they give out. Kind people are usually treated kindly. Generous people usually have generosity shown to them. Liars get lied to. Servants eventually get served. Encouragers get encouraged, etc. Once again, if you are honest, you must admit this principle that Jesus taught has as much direct connection to us as it did to the hearers in those moments so long ago.

Literally, thousands upon thousands of examples could be given from the pages of Scripture. The Bible consists of sixty-six books written by approximately forty authors over a period of 1,600 years. Most of those forty authors were uneducated ordinary people. In fact, the only writers of Scripture that were well educated were Moses[97], Solomon[98], Luke[99], and Paul the Apostle.[100] The rest were just "regular" everyday people. From farmers to shepherds to fisherman, they were not sharp enough people in their own intellect, training, and abilities to assemble a collection of books that would change the lives of millions, possibly billions over several millennia of time. How can writings of such people over such a vast span of time have the same unified theme and, when properly understood, contain not one contradiction? How can literature with this somewhat sketchy crowd of writers explain everything from the origins of the world and the creation of the human race to how history will close? What other book foretells happenings centuries before they even occur with such amazing and miniscule accuracy? What other sacred book has such principles that span the centuries to help people in every time, place, and culture?

This is why Bible-teaching churches are so incredibly relevant. It is because they believe, teach, and sincerely attempt to connect the principles in those writings to people's every day lives. Frankly, that isn't really all that difficult. I have been reading the Bible in a variety of translations and versions for more than three decades, and I am continually amazed at the timelessness of it. It has advice on how to handle your finances, how to make wise business choices, how to avoid adultery and being trapped in life-controlling habits. It advises on parenting, marital harmony, cosigning a loan, handling arguments, avoiding conflict, controlling one's temper, planning for the future, leaving an inheritance for your grandkids, etc. I am not kidding when I state the list is almost endless.

The same issues that humanity struggled with from the beginning are the same issues you and I struggle with today and that every person has throughout the annals of human history. As if that were not enough, the principles contained within this sacred book transcend time and culture and are still apropos today in innumerable ways and situations. Please sincerely ask yourself how could that be without the superintendence of a divine being?

Friend, if you are looking for a place that provides relevant advice and assistance for your day-to-day life and authentic caring friends to help you understand how to live out that counsel, you simply could not find a more relevant place to be than a Bible-believing, Bible-teaching church!

UNDENIABLE SINCERITY

I hate phoniness. I am from the northeast region of the United States, and some say we are too direct. However, one of the things I appreciate about my culture is the no-nonsense demeanor of the people. Granted, some express that directness in a rude way, and I certainly do not appreciate that any more than anyone else.

Yet I have lived in and visited other parts of my country, and one of my biggest struggles has been what we New Englanders would call incessant beating around the bush. In other words, saying what one does not genuinely mean or saying one thing but meaning another. I once heard a Southern comedian sarcastically say, "When you ask a Northerner 'how are you?' they will *tell* you."

While I understand no one wants to hear another spill their guts every time they are asked, I would respond, "Why ask if you do not really want to know?" If you do not really care to know, do not ask. To ask but not really care, or even worse, to get upset if they actually answer your question seems phony or at the very least insincere. While there are always exceptions, the vast majority of people I have met and come to call my friends in the church world are the most sincere people I have ever known. With all the warts and fumbles I have witnessed and been guilty of myself, there is still an unmistakable heartfelt sincerity that undergirds everything that is done and said in the life of a devored Christ follower.

In the mid-1980s, the church I attended was privileged enough to host the then famous Christian rock band, Mylon LeFevre and Broken Heart at our local high school auditorium. As a young man raised with a taste for bands like KISS, Alice Cooper, and the like, it was so exciting to discover that there was similar music that existed but with a Christian message!

I remember when they took the stage to loud rock music and a great light show complete with smoke and pyrotechnics! In the midst of the concert, Mylon often shared thoughts from the Bible and what the lyrics meant in the songs they wrote. At that time, I was not aware of his background. I was amazed when he told of his conversion to Christianity and the life he led before. As a fairly successful rock musician, Mylon used to make $50,000 a night! Of course, his spiritual rebirth gave him a new set of convictions, and the Lord redirected him out of that arena at that time.

He then told story of how he had obtained a position in the local school in the Atlanta area as a janitor. He went from making $50K a night to $75 a week! He was complaining to the Lord about that one day while he was on his hands and knees scrubbing the gymnasium floor. He heard the Lord gently but firmly whisper, "Who are you doing this for?" Mylon's attitude immediately changed, and he scrubbed that floor and got it the cleanest he possibly could...with a toothbrush!

Okay, think about that for a minute. A successful musician goes from making big bucks along with all the bells and whistles of being a rock star to scrubbing a school floor with a toothbrush for $75 a week. Who would do such a thing? Not someone who just got *some religion*, but someone who had a genuine encounter with the living God of the Bible. Only someone with great conviction, dedication, and deep sincerity in their attempt to honor the God who changed their heart! Though I must admit, this level of sincerity is unusual, even in the church, it exemplifies what many sincere followers demonstrate. Most of us will never be or do what Mylon did, but let me share another example a little more on the level of most of us.

During an eight-month interim between pastorates, my family and I had the unique pleasure of attending what our family has come to call the greatest church on the planet—James River Church in Ozark, Missouri. This church started with about seventy people with a pastor who was not very successful (to say the least) with a church planting attempt in Overland Park, Kansas. In a matter of five years, the church blossomed to over three thousand people. With Pastors John and Debbie Lindell at the helm, after having planted at least three other successful churches, they also launched their second campus, not long after, with well over twelve thousand people in attendance. The success of this church in the very buckle of the Bible belt with over six hundred churches within a forty-five-minute drive of it is nothing short of miraculous. A large percentage of that number are new converts, by the way. James River is a genuine, sweet, and unmistakable sovereign move of God.

Now you may wonder why I shared that. Anyone who leads anything, be it a business venture or ministry, that has *that* level of success is prone to arrogance. Success is a funny thing. It will test the mettle of who a person really is. Make no mistake about it. Who a person really is deep inside will always surface eventually. I have seen men and women with far less success than the Lindell's develop into prideful, power-hungry, people-using, insincere jerks. (There's that northeast directness again. Like I said, the real person always surfaces, like it or not!) Unless you have been living in a cave for the past twenty-five years, you have seen people whose rise to influence and success has led them to care more about themselves then their original mission to serve.

All that to tell you about what I witnessed one Sunday morning in the atrium of James River Church while I served as a greeter. The church had just shifted to three services to accommodate the enormous growth of the congregation, and it was during a

CHURCH! WHO NEEDS IT?!

time where there was no traffic in that huge foyer. There was very little movement at all, and what I saw was probably unnoticed by anyone else but the Lord and me, yet it so impressed me that it is indelibly etched in my mind.

Debbie Lindell was being her usual sweet-spirited self as she made her way through the atrium, stopping to chat with and encourage all the various team members working there. Shortly after that, I happened to look over as she walked by a rather obscure part of that huge foyer where no one was and no one would see. Then I watched her do what few successful people would ever do at the pinnacle of their success—she bent down, picked up a small barely noticeable candy wrapper, and walked to a trash receptacle and threw it away. All around this first lady of the church were volunteers who would gladly have done that for her, but she did not need to ask anyone. Why? Because in her heart of hearts, she is a servant, and a deeply sincere one at that. There may well be people with that kind of sincerity outside of the church of Jesus Christ, but I have never met one.

My experience has taught me that few people are that selfless. Many people's seemingly benevolent actions have some level of ulterior motives behind them. Whether it's a desire for recognition, a need to simply feel good about themselves, or for something else they are going to get as a result of their good deed, it seems to me that precious few are so sincere in their acts of kindness that they want nothing *whatsoever* in return. The only place I have witnessed that level of sincerity is in the followers of Jesus who are attached to a local Bible-believing church. Though none of us really knows the heart, for every apparent insincere person you could find in the church world, I can take you to at least a hundred who, from every indicator, have the level of sincerity I have mentioned—you know, kind of like Jesus!

UNEQUALED WHOLENESS

Life is full of broken people. If you have ever been a resident in my native southern New England, and maybe even if you have not, you may have heard of Boston's "Combat Zone." If you have not, suffice to say, it is a very wild place. From porn shops, peep shows, and prostitutes to rampant drugs and drunkards, you cannot walk more than a hundred yards without witnessing human life in its most depraved state.

In my pre-Christian days of prodigal living, I visited the Combat Zone more than once. Pardon the crassness, but I can still remember walking by an inebriated man lying on the edge of the sidewalk with a puddle of urine under his groin area. Even in my depraved state, I was saddened by the sight, and I wondered what could lead someone to such a broken existence. Fast-forward about a decade…

The church I was part of through the eighties and most of the nineties occasionally held outdoor services under a big tent. The idea was to bring the church to the nonchurchgoer. It was kind of a neat concept of yesteryear (mostly). We saw many, *many* broken people wander in under that big top over the years. We saw many of them discover the reality of a God who loved them so much, even in their defiant sinful condition, to wrap His loving arms around them and joyfully welcome them into his family. However, there is one man who stands out in my mind's eye.

Paul was a cocaine addict. The night he came to the tent meeting, he could barely stand up. I can still see him holding onto one of the large tent ropes to steady himself. He had shoulder-length hair and glassy, bloodshot, empty eyes that seemed to point to the emptiness in his soul. He stayed for the worship service, listened to the loud contemporary music, and heard some really good teaching from the Bible. That night, my pastor was on the phone with him until two in the morning, trying to convince him not to pull the trigger of the gun that was pointed at his head while they spoke. When they hung up, my pastor was convinced that Paul would kill himself and there was not a thing anyone could do to stop him. The pastor was wrong.

Paul showed up the next night again and asked Jesus Christ to forgive his sins, come into his life, and make something of the mess he has made of it. He was desperate and knew he needed divine intervention. Though it may be uncomfortable to be in that condition, it is not a bad place to be. God does His best work in seemingly hopeless and impossible situations. When we come to the end of ourselves, we come to the beginning of God, if (and that's a big if) we are willing to surrender control to Him. Paul was. Jesus changed his life in an unmistakable way. Our church helped Paul go to a Christ-centered rehabilitation program in Michigan called Teen Challenge,[101] and the metamorphosis that transpired was both incredible and fascinating. Let me tell you a little about this ministry by going back near its inception.

In the late 1950s, there was a ministry in rural Pennsylvania that was claiming a 70 percent cure rate for drug addicts and alcoholics. The assertion was that the people who came through their program were still clean five years after completing it. The government's best psychologists and psychiatrists could not produce even close to a 5 percent cure rate. So our government spent tens of thousands of dollars to research it and prove them wrong, and they did just that. Teen Challenge was not producing a 70 percent cure rate; in fact, their cure rate was actually an astounding 86 percent![102] Over the years, this amazing ministry blossomed, and now has facilities all over the globe. It still has the highest cure rate of any rehabilitation program on the entire earth. That's where we sent Paul.

Six months later, he came to our church on a visit from Michigan. I did not even recognize him at first. Now its not that the style or type of clothes he wore or the length of his hair made him (or anyone else) any holier. However, he looked like a completely different person—that's because he was! He stood straight and tall at the pulpit with his suit and tie on. But the most noticeable thing was the hope in his entire demeanor. He spoke with confidence and assurance of how Jesus had taken the pieces of his broken life and put them all together perfectly. He was then studying to be a pastor because he was so in love with the God who was so in love with him—a broken wreck of a human being. Though Paul is a dramatic example, I have seen Jesus bring wholeness to thousands of people over the years now, most of whom had seemingly ordinary lives but still sensed a deep emptiness inside. I am one of them.

My journey was not as severe as Paul's, though it sure seemed it at times. Though, as I shared earlier in this book, my first encounter with Christ did not occur in a congregation or church, I affirm that the wholeness I discovered in a close relationship with Jesus was not complete until I got anchored to a local church. When I came to faith in Christ as a young machinist in 1981, my union went on strike just a short time later. I was out of work but still had enough income to pay my bills and live fairly well. This stretch went on for about ten months. I was led to believe in that early stage that a Christ-follower really did not need church per se. To a former late-night bar hopper and night clubber, the idea of getting up early to go to church on a day off never sounded very inviting, so I happily received that theology!

During those ten months out of work, I read my Bible and prayed about three to four hours per day. As you can imagine, with that level of intense hunger and free time, I became well-grounded in my understanding of the Bible and in my relationship to the Lord. That was fine for a while, but I could sense there was still something not quite right. It was not until about a year into my newfound faith that I really came to see my need for the local church.

I started to attend a local Assemblies of God church where I came to experience the presence of God at a much-deeper level. People utilized their spiritual gifts in the congregation, and I was genuinely and profoundly touched, particularly when the prophetic[103] was in operation. I never experienced those things studying my Bible at home.

At that local church, I met people more experienced in the things of God who helped me understand many things about life and godliness I could not have discovered on my own. I received support of various kinds through difficult times; support I knew nothing of during that one year on my own. Many of the friendships that I forged during that particular season of my life are still vibrant and active now over three decades later. There is a connection that is made to the body of Christ that births wholeness, which churchless believers can never know, and that is by God's own design.

That wholeness is not found by watching preachers on TV, nor by showing up at the building on Christmas or Easter out of guilt, tradition, or to impress God. It is not found by weekly attendees who avoid involvement, nor by those who avoid building relationships with godly people. It is not found by professing believers who hop, shop, and bop to whatever church really seems to appeal to them or has "the Spirit moving." Neither is it found in any *lasting* or *corporate* way by Christian thrill-seekers.[104]

It is critical to understand this next statement: the local church is not humanity's idea but God's. He has established it as His primary avenue of accomplishing the mission that Jesus has given to His followers—that is to "make disciples."[105] A disciple is a lifelong learner and adherent to the teachings of another. In this case, that would be Jesus Christ. Throughout the New Testament, it becomes clear that local congregations are where that happens *best*. I have noticed that many professing believers who avoid a strong, dedicated connection to a local church struggle with gaining a genuine godly contentment. Though all believers struggle with sin, they often seem trapped and unable to escape. Though believers who are faithful and dedicated to their church struggle as well, my observation has been that it is not at the same depth or level. There is a simple explanation for that.

John the Beloved wrote some very interesting and helpful words in one of his letters. In 1 John chapter 1, he stated, "If we walk in the light, as He [Jesus] is in the light, we have fellowship with one another, and the blood of Jesus, His Son, purifies us from all sin." Allow me to paraphrase what he is saying:

> If we continue in a close relationship with Jesus in the light of His love and guidance, we will develop ongoing genuine friendships with other believers and in the midst of those relationships, the blood of Jesus will be more fully applied to our lives and we will be purified from patterns of sin that cause us pain and hardship.

That does not happen by watching church on TV. Electronic avenues of spiritual food are just *supplements* to what God intended to happen through the local church. *Wholeness* is a by-product of *holiness* and that is developed to the highest degree in close relationship with the community of God's people and a strong network of mutual accountability.

Where did the transformation of that man Paul begin? At a ministry effort put out by a local church. From a pastor and congregation, which had experienced the wholeness only the God of the Bible can give and spent time, money, and manpower to get out into the community to tell them about it. When did my wholeness and that of countless others develop and mature best? In a local church with committed Bible-believing fellow strugglers all under the caring guidance of our pastors and leadership. In the presence of God, we "spur one another on toward love and good deeds."[106] We pray for one another in difficult times. We develop friendships, and in the midst of them, we discover who we can trust enough to confess our struggles to. Thus we "confess [our] sins to each other and pray for each other so that [we] may be healed."[107]

Though these things are the ideal and not every church has this level of authenticity, many do. You will find wholeness in the congregations that do like no other place on the planet. I do not say that as a matter of theory or from something I read in a book or from something someone else told me. I have walked in the experience of it myself for over three decades. In addition, I have seen many, many others walk in it as well. That wholeness awaits all who will come wholeheartedly to Him and connect well with His people.

UNCOMPETITIVE SERVANTS

Gay rights. Women's rights. Reproductive rights. A plethora of groups in our society are ever chanting about some kind of rights they feel they have or are entitled to. They write letters to people in authority, voice their complaints on talk shows, or wave picket signs at unsuspecting motorists as they drive by. Of course, there *is* a time to stand up against oppression and speak up for what is right. However, when was the last time you saw anyone, *anyone*, mind you, fight for their *responsibilities*? Have you ever wondered why so many people are insistent on getting what they *want* as opposed to helping others get what they *need*?

Can I be candid? Our focus, particularly in the West, is typically ourselves and our own need for advancement. So much so that people with a genuine servant's heart really stand out. I mentioned a few already but, after being part of the church world so long, it really isn't hard for me to think of many more.

We started a brand-new church in January of 2010. Ocean Community Christian Church had her grand opening on January 10 at the Westerly Middle School in Westerly, Rhode Island (my home state). That day is etched in my memory forever. Besides the relational connections made at our small coffee bar, and the great worship, we gave away a bike to a little girl, an iPod Nano to a teenager, and dinner for two to an adult. Seeing the crowd that came, many of whom I had never met, was both the ending and the beginning of a great journey. The majority of those who gathered that day had no idea what it took to get that church started, but my family and all the team sure did!

The first meetings began an entire year prior with about twenty-five people. We held a couple of public meetings in Westerly in January 2009 to gauge the interest level and need of people. Among a list of other things, our launch team came out in the cold with homemade baked goodies and set up the room to greet everyone with a warm smile. Their eagerness and anticipation was so refreshing.

From there, we began to hold leadership meetings primarily in a couple of homes, though we occasionally did so in restaurants and even in a bowling alley! Again, team members brought baked goods, beverages, and other items to make the time fun. They read three leadership books and listened to me teach about them in our discussion time. This team that had grown to thirty-seven over the next few months was challenged to come to Westerly (where most of them did not live) for errands and entertainment for the express purpose of meeting local people. They would then bring as many names of those people as they could to add to a prayer list so our team could pray for them at our weekly meetings. This small team of thirty-seven people (of which only twenty-two were adults) gathered six hundred fifty names by the time the church started!

A couple of months later, we began to hold discussion groups for seekers in the local public schools at night. Again, the same things had to be done—setting up rooms, bringing in and setting up for refreshments, being ready to minister to people however they needed, on and on. All of this while the weekly leadership meetings and assignments continued.

Then we had to plan and promote our preview services building up to the grand opening. This often included taking fliers and passing them out any and every place we could think to put them. Charlie, our worship leader, had to gather musicians, put together a musical repertoire for the team to begin to practice, and then meet with them regularly to prepare. He and Chad our sound and technical hero discussed and advised me as to what we needed for sound and electronic equipment, then they went out and obtained the vast majority of it. Candidly, I do not know what I would have done without these two guys and their families!

Then the preview services kicked into gear—once a month including one on Christmas Eve when most people would rather be with their families to continue their traditions. On the two weekends before the grand opening (or launch as many of us called it) we went door to door to pass out 1500 door hangers. This took our teams many hours of walking, which they tirelessly did without complaining! Even after someone called the police on us, and we were told not to do that in our target city, this team willingly moved out to the surrounding towns to continue spreading the word and inviting anyone and everyone they possibly could.

All of this required the shifting of work schedules and vacation dates, as well as giving up an enormous amount of time. Some of our launch team members returned to other churches after they got us off the ground, so to speak. However, the majority continued this rigorous routine. Every single Sunday, we had to carry in thousands of dollars of sound equipment, coffee shop–style tables and chairs to set up the coffee bar plus continue to bake, as well as donate, those goodies. All that in addition to weekly worship practices and the use of their time, talents, treasures, and tithes to support all that God was doing.

Because of a zoning issue, we were forced to get our own facility just four months after the grand opening at the school. The launch team members who stayed with us, in addition to the weekly rigors already described for Sunday mornings then spent the next few months working to renovate a store front that we were to rent. This required hours and hours of time (after they were done at their paying jobs) of demolition, cleaning, building, and preparation of that new "home." Again, they did all this tirelessly, at great personal sacrifice, and without complaining![108]

Here's another example.

Larry is an Elvis impersonator. His apartment walls are covered with Elvis paraphernalia. A single dad, he also has a withered hand and arm from an accident in his younger years. Many people in his condition would seek to receive government help by being categorized as disabled. Not Larry.

At three years into the ministry of our church, we expanded into the storefront across the parking lot where our church was. Part of our desire was to provide something for the teens and children of our church and community. We decided to develop that storefront for such things. Frankly, it was very difficult to get much help from our people. That's when Larry really rose to the surface.

Sort of a jack-of-all-trades, Larry began advising our building team on how we could best develop that family center and spend the least amount of money doing so. Over the next two months, he logged far more time stripping floors, laying down tile and rubber flooring, spackling walls, and painting than anyone else in our church. Twelve-to-fourteen-hour days became common. He arranged his entire life around that project and almost single-handedly completed the majority of the work needed for us to open on Easter Sunday. He did all that with a disabled arm, working around the care of his ten-year-old daughter without a single complaint. When I went to hand him a gift card to a restaurant as a small token of appreciation, I had to talk him into taking it.

Why did I just tell you all of that? To illustrate what servants are really like. All that this team did, that some *continued* to do, and all that Larry did was done voluntarily. Not only did no one get rich, no one was even getting paid at all. Getting paid? Are you kidding! They actually *paid* to do what they did!

Why in the world would anyone make all those sacrifices for a volunteer organization from which they gain no tangible or monetary advantage? Well, either they are crazy, they feel some kind of divine compulsion, or both. These are servants, and that is what the church is made up of. Oh, I know not everyone who attends religious gatherings has this kind of heart, but many, if not most, really do. When they know there is a genuine need, they rise to the challenge. This is just one team that I described. After many years of ministry experience in the local church, I could share hundreds of similar stories. Frankly, finding that kind of selfless, humble servitude from people *not looking for anything in return*[109] is rare to find at least outside the confines of a group of Bible-believing Christ followers.

UNSEEN GENEROSITY

"He's blind in that eye. It was nothing you did, and there isn't a thing you can do about it. Unless there's a miracle, your son will never see out of that eye." This is one of many painful statements the doctor made to my wife and me on March 9, 1998. That was the day our family dynamic would change forever. Our youngest son Ezra Samuel was born with three rare conditions—multiple birth defects (including blindness in his right eye), mental retardation and, as we would discover over time, three behavioral disorders. We did not know of any of this until the day he was born. There were no indicators or warning during the pregnancy.

Please be assured we love our son more than we could ever explain. We would not trade him for all the money in the world. However, the issues that come with caring for him and dealing with him in our day-to-day life are so stressful that it is near impossible for anyone to really comprehend unless they have lived with him for more than a week. In fact, some people get annoyed when we try to explain as if they somehow know exactly what should be done to fix our situation. So much for the advice of the highly educated and experienced experts plus tireless efforts of two battle-weary parents!

The term *special needs* can encompass too many scenarios to list. Anyone who has a child with this level of needs understands that it is rare for the care of two special-needs people to be near the same. Those who babysit them, care for them, or interact with them still, at the end of the day, get to go home, typically to a fairly normal life.

My niece and her husband have four biological children. Three of them have special needs of one level or another. They have also adopted three of their nephews to rescue them from a difficult home life. Some years ago, she began to tell me about a retreat for families affected by disabilities and what an enormous relief it was for her and her family. This ministry was born from the heart of a woman named Joni Erickson Tada,[110] who herself became a paraplegic as a result of a diving accident when she was just sixteen.[111]

I am thankful that my niece's gentle persistence convinced us to go. It was one of the greatest weeks of our lives. A short-term missionary was assigned to Ezra from the minute he woke up till he went to bed, though we still saw him and ate with him all week. They had special events for Ezra's big brothers, Seth and Caleb who endure the stress all year long. They provided special seminars and events for my wife Theresa and me. What a relief! What a blessing!

"Nice story, but what has any of this got to do with generosity?" you may ask. Well, let me explain. I would love to tell you that going to such an event is free. Far from it, nor could it (or should it) be. Frankly, without help, one would have to be quite well to do to be able to attend, especially if they had a large family. That first year, we simply made the director for the retreats in Spruce Lake, Pennsylvania, aware of our need. Shortly thereafter, we received notice that someone we did not even know, had never even met, would cover almost half the cost for our family of five totaling several hundreds of dollar! Someone else we had never met donated another hundred and fifty dollars! My understanding is that neither of these folks is any more financially secure than we were.

At the close of our first "Joni and friends" family retreat, we registered immediately for the following year. We put down a small deposit to be sure we would have that settled. We already knew that it was somewhat cost prohibitive for our family, but we knew we simply had to be there.

Fast forward a year. I was sent out by Seaport Community Church in Groton, Connecticut (where I was the executive pastor) to start the previously mentioned new church in my home state of Rhode Island.

Now, contrary to what some may believe, most ministers do not make much money, but God has always graciously taken care of us. My family likes to eat as much as any other family. My two older sons developed "hollow-leg syndrome" about the age of twelve, and they can pack in a lot of food. We still have bills to pay like everyone else. We have dreams for our kids that include college, graduate schools, and more. We need a special trust set up for our special needs son to be taken care of after we are gone from this earth. Banks and landlords do not care if we had a powerful church service or people came to faith or not. They just want their money.

All those comments to point out that we need *the green stuff* just like nonminister's families. The problem is that our mother church[112] was no wealthier than any other church. How would they help us financially? They helped as much as they could, but by the time we started the church, my salary was less than half of what I made as a senior pastor in Missouri—*less than half.*

To try to help us raise the $1,500 for our family to go, I simply sent out an e-mail to several pastors and Christian friends that I know, explaining our need. That was it; no pressure, no fundraising letters, no follow up phone calls, just a single e-mail. Within two weeks, we had one church in Missouri send us five hundred dollars, another in Providence, Rhode Island, send us two hundred fifty dollars, a friend sent one hundred, and another sent one hundred and fifty. That is two-thirds of our total costs from that one e-mail.

Both of those churches have needy people of their own to help and plenty of bills, I am sure. The friends who sent us financial support each have families of their own and expenses like everyone. Most people will never know their names and, frankly, they could not care less. No one has seen their acts of generosity, and it does not matter to them at all. They did not do what they did to be noticed or applauded by people. I do not even think they necessarily do it to please God, although that is certainly the cry of their heart. I believe they do it because it has become the expression of who they are. Better yet, the expression of *whose* they are.

As I have already mentioned, we had just started a new church. This is no small task. Thankfully, the fellowship that I have ministerial credentials with (the Assemblies of God) has a great plan in place to help church planters get started. The charge from the elders in my denomination was to raise $15,000 toward the startup costs, which would demonstrate to them that we "had what it takes" to start something from scratch. Our district office would then match that $15,000 with another $15,000 to $20,000. This would then qualify us for a no-interest, pay-it-forward $30,000 loan from our national office. So off we went.

The same church that helped us get to the Joni and Friends retreat previously donated $2,500 toward that $15,000. Another church gave us $1,800, and one church of less than one hundred people gave us $6,000! That is only the churches where the majority of the attendees do not even know me well, if at all.

As for individuals, one couple took the proceeds from the sale of some property and gave us a large undisclosed amount, while one single gal in the military gave us $7,500! This is only *some* of the people who helped us. It was truly amazing. The generosity of God's people is astounding to me and reveals a motivator that transcends this world.

The old saying "look out for number one" is no less true in our society today than it was years ago. So what causes someone to give away large sums of money, at times to total strangers, when they have their own bills to pay? What motivates a heart to help others when they themselves have their own needs? Well, I realize that there could be many possible reasons (some good and some not so much). However, my experience affirms that this kind of selfless generosity is most often the expression of a heart that has known immense generosity, i.e., from the forgiven followers of Jesus Christ.

They have experienced the curiously amazing mercy of the only One who truly knows the heart and could thus rightly judge it. Somehow, He has seen fit to lavish His generous unmerited forgiveness upon them. They have sweetly received the exact opposite of what their deeds, attitudes, and motives deserved, and now their hearts overflow with that same generosity. Further, they have seen His faithfulness in the practical matters of life so that they lack for nothing they truly need.

Psalm 34:9–10 states:

> Fear the Lord, you His godly people,
> for those who fear Him will have all they need.
> Even strong young lions sometimes go hungry,
> but those who trust in the Lord will lack no good thing.

*   *   *

The handwritten return address was from Kentucky. I do not know a soul in the Bluegrass State! I read the name and had no idea who it was. *Why was this person writing to me?* I wondered. I opened the envelope, assuming it was some kind of marketing campaign from a company who had somehow found our address. What I found instead was a letter and a check for $550 toward our new youth and family center! I was overjoyed and perplexed. The generous donor mentioned that he had attended our mother church in Groton, Connecticut. I called the pastor and told him about it. He had no idea who the person was. Of course, I sent a handwritten note of gratitude to this generous man and his wife in Kentucky.

Two months later, I received another letter with the same handwritten return address. I opened it up and discovered a letter with a prayer request and more contact info for this kind couple. Also, there was another generous check, but this one was for $1,000! I e-mailed the man and stayed in contact with him for some time.

So let's think about this. A man and his wife who I have never met and has never attended our church but visited our mother church has sent us over $1,500 toward a youth and family center he knows nothing about and will probably never see. How many stories like *that* do you know of by personal experience outside of the church? What incredible generosity!

Now I know that there are exceptions. There are certainly plenty of stingy people in the church world. Let me remind you again that being in church no more makes a person a Christ follower than being in a garage makes one a car. If one among the followers of Jesus seems stingy, there are only a few possibilities. First, they may not truly be a follower of Jesus, but someone who is religious, a seeker who has not truly committed their life to Christ, or just an attendee without dedication. Secondly, the person may not genuinely grasp how awful sin is in the eyes of God and, thus, not really understand just how generous He has been to them. Thirdly, they may have not matured to this level in their spiritual journey. Lastly, they may simply not have the resources.

All that being said, generally speaking, God's people are generous because their God is. From cheerfully paying their tithes (a full ten percent of their income) to their local church (as th Bible instructs), to giving offerings above that to missionaries, widows, orphans, and others in need, God's people are generous like no other I have ever known or observed. Typically, this is not so people will think highly of them or to gain points with God. Know the generosity of God through the kind and giving hearts of His children. Connect with a good church!

UNBIASED VARIETY

I love ice cream. However, with a couple of heart conditions, I try not to indulge too often as it can greatly increase one's bad cholesterol. If I could just live in an area without a Cold Stone ice cream parlor, I think I could do better! Every time I drive by one, it takes some serious self-control not to stop and treat myself to some or maybe a *lot* of it.

I am always a little overwhelmed when I first walk in. Besides the specials listed on the wall in the area for customers, there is the message menu behind the counter. The list of flavors, gourmet treats, and the various combinations, sizes, and toppings—my mouth is watering just writing about it! While I like having many options, I must admit, ordering would be easier, clearer, and faster if there were fewer of them. However, that would mean less delicious variety to tantalize my taste buds.

This is a good illustration of the church world, especially for those who were not brought up in a particular denomination or tradition. The seeker decides he or she is interested in understanding more about Christianity. One of the first logical places they will explore to fulfill that desire is a church. However, with so many different kinds of churches and a plethora of denominational names, they wonder, "Which one do I go to? Is one the *right* one? If so, does that mean the others are the *wrong* ones? How can you tell which is a good church? Why are there so many?" They even wonder if the followers of Jesus are *that* confused, why even check out their place of worship?

This struggle is not unique to the nonchurched seeker or skeptic either. I do not even know how many Christ followers I have heard bash denominations as if a unified approach to spiritual life and ministry is somehow frowned upon by God! That being said, I do understand because I too used to see them as a blemish on the reputation of the church. However, I no longer see them that way. The word *denomination* comes from the Latin word *dēnōminātiō* and refers to "a calling by name."[113]

In the Apostle Paul's first letter to the Christ followers in the ancient city of Corinth, he was trying to correct them for fighting with each other and splitting into factions. This was not much of an example of the humble Christ to the non-Christian world around them! In chapter 1 of that letter and verses 10–17, he speaks sternly to them for defining their spiritual views and pursuits under the *name* of a primary Christian *leader*. Some have taken this further than the Holy Spirit seems to have intended and said it is wrong to have a group of Christians be defined under a name.

However, it is critical to understand that Christian denominations do not typically define themselves, nor have they determined their particular name, as that under a particular *person*.[114] Those that *have* professed such a thing have rarely been seen as orthodox in their approach to God, are not typically accepted as part of true Christendom, and often end up in radical practices and heretical teachings. Rather, their denominational name simply helps them clarify their doctrine, particular focus and governing polity. This is a far cry from what Paul was correcting the Corinthians for. Let's consider those things briefly and the need as well as the benefit to having a denominational persuasion.

To be fair and clear, those who insist that people must be part of their denomination, exclude other Christ followers who do not agree with them, and do not rejoice at the successes of other churches are operating in a wrong spirit. *That* is what Paul was correcting. Also, let me say that nondenominational churches also define who they are, where they are heading, and how they will be governed. The irony is that some nondenominational people bash those in denominations and act in the very spirit that motivated them to resist denominations in the first place!

First of all, what is doctrine and how important is it to a church? Doctrine can be defined as "a body or system of teachings relating to a particular subject."[115] Basically, doctrine is a clear system of belief. It is the understanding of truth that a person(s) or group has upon which to base the application of those professed realities. Of course, as in many other areas of life, there are some beliefs that are more critical than others even though both play their part. For example, the doctrine of salvation (how one gets to heaven) is obviously more important than how often a particular church partakes in communion. One's belief as to whether the Bible is inspired by God or not is far more critical than what style of worship music should be played during a religious service or celebration.

The doctrines that are considered the most critical to a denomination (or church) are typically called "cardinal doctrines." Certainly, someone who was looking for a church home would want to be sure that the place they are attending is in agreement with their own belief system. Why would anyone frequent any type of meetings where they are in disagreement with what is conveyed? Having a denominational name can help people to determine if they want to attend that church or not.

Secondly, many denominations are known for a particular focus. For instance, Southern Baptist Churches (among many others) are typically strong on Bible teaching and evangelism (sharing the gospel with non-followers). Pentecostal churches are known for exuberant worship and the expression of the spiritual gifts spoken of in the New Testament. So if one has a particular persuasion in any of those areas, the denominational title helps them decide where to attend.

Thirdly, wherever money is donated, time is volunteered, and people are asked to follow leadership, there needs to be an agreed upon system of government. This is no different in the religious world. In the Christian world, there are various systems of church government. The most common three systems of government are (though some use a combination of them):

1. *Episcopalian.* This involves a hierarchy of leaders with the primary leadership responsibility of a local assembly of members resting in a bishop. They are typically overseen by a group of spiritual elders whose primary leadership is as a bishop (examples are the Roman Catholic church and Eastern Orthodox churches).
2. *Congregational.* The name communicates this system well. It appeared after the Protestant Reformation and may well have been somewhat of a reaction to what was seen as an overbearing hierarchy. Here the congregation is seen as the highest governing body as opposed to elders, pastors, bishops, or the like. They see each local church as autonomous. Voting is a high priority in these churches (examples would be the Baptist Church and the United Church of Christ).
3. *Presbyterian. Presbytery* refers to a group of spiritual elders similar to a committee except with much more authority. That presbytery is usually made up of credentialed ministers but can also include lay leaders (of course the most obvious example would be the Presbyterian Church).[116]

Within every family tree are multiple smaller nuclei of relatives. Each one has their own personality, practices, hobbies, likes, dislikes, etc., and yet they are still part of the greater tree. They are still part of the family. While most families may have a certain level of disagreement, if they are a *healthy* family, they agree on some major (cardinal) beliefs they hold to. Aren't the parallels obvious?

We all know that within every denomination, there are sincere (as well as insincere) people. There are those who genuinely hold to the cardinal beliefs of biblical Christianity (those that effect salvation *primarily* though not *exclusively*), and there are those who do not. When Christ followers get to their final eternal destination, there will not be separate sections for different denominations but one church. Frankly, God sees just one body with each individual and denomination as members of that body. Each denomination will discover where they were right and where they were not. Until then, we live in a finite fallen world, and our understanding is limited and even somewhat darkened. Because of all these factors, doesn't it only make sense that there would be a variety within the family of God?

Clearly, God has not withdrawn His hand of blessing on churches that align with a denomination. The sovereign God does not bless what He deems as wrong or sinful. That suggests that, at the very least, He is not opposed to them.

One other thought pertains to what we call communion or the Lord's Supper. In that practice ordained by the Lord Himself on the night He was betrayed, He took bread and broke it to symbolize how His body was to be broken for us. Could it be that what is often seen as a break in the body of Christ, which is to exemplify the relationships between Jesus and His bride, actually illustrates that broken body even further? Does this frailty and perceived brokenness not communicate even louder that the broken are welcome? I think it does. The variety of these expressions of God can actually help people find the best spot in which they feel the most proper fit. What's wrong with that?

You may have heard the old saying, "Variety is the spice of life." I submit to you, it's the same in the church. Instead of embracing a distaste for this, I encourage you to find the *flavor* of the body of Christ that suits you best (in the light of your biblical understanding) and savor it. Enjoy!

6

THE QUESTIONS

In my opinion, pop theology leaves more questions than it provides answers. A spiritual system of beliefs that professes to honor the God of the Bible would surely agree with the Bible of that God. And yet as we consider the way that many professing believers live out their supposed faith, a variety of questions are implied that really need to be answered. Since we are talking about the God of the Bible, it only makes consistent sense that the answers to those questions should agree with that revelation. Let's consider some of those questions in this chapter in the light of biblical teaching.

CAN'T I JUST WORSHIP GOD AT HOME?

This is the most pronounced question and implication from the life of many. Therefore, we may commit more ink and paper to consider it than the others.

* * *

As I was opening the front door of our storefront church plant one bright spring Sunday morning, a man who runs a business in the same plaza cheerfully rode up on his bike. He wanted to give me some brochures for his services in hopes that I would promote his business to our congregation. In a couple of previous conversations, he had asserted that he was a believer. I invited him in to join us for worship that was to begin in a couple of hours.

With a big smile on his face, he waved his extended arm toward the beautiful sunshiny sky and proudly proclaimed, "I can worship God out here!" Of course, that is true, but to be candid, I doubt that's *really* what he had in mind when he jumped on his bike that morning.

Another day, as I was driving down the main strip of our town, I spotted a rather interesting bumper sticker. It read, "Nature is my church." This puts forth the same basic idea, *I can worship God anywhere I please and don't have to be part of a church to do it.* Again, while that may be a popular idea, if we're talking about the God of the Bible, we need to ask, "Is that really what that God intended for His followers?"

We know from Scripture that the Almighty God of the Scriptures is omnipresent (meaning everywhere present at the same time). In Psalm 139, David, the King of Israel, wrote,

I can never escape from Your Spirit!
I can never get away from Your presence [emphasis added]!
If I go up to heaven, You are there;
if I go down to the grave, You are there.
If I ride the wings of the morning,
if I dwell by the farthest oceans,
even there Your hand will guide me,
and Your strength will support me.
I could ask the darkness to hide me
and the light around me to become night—
but even in darkness I cannot hide from You.
To You the night shines as bright as day.

Unfortunately, an understanding of a *characteristic* of God does not always lead to a proper *theology* about His will. Since God is everywhere, the short answer to question number one in this chapter is certainly a resounding yes! Since He is everywhere, He can be worshipped anywhere. Cool! However, the real question is, does the God of the Bible give any instruction or indication that private worship can replace public worship? If we had a scale with one side labeled Private Worship and the other labeled Public Worship, which side would the lifestyles and modes of worship purported in God's Word place more weight on? Is this an "either/or" question, or is the answer more of a "both/and" one? Consider the following:

The first couple Adam and Eve had many children. Their first three were sons and were called Cain, Abel, and Seth. Seth means *granted* for God had granted the first couple another son to take the place of Abel whom Cain had killed (more on that later in this chapter).

It wasn't until Seth grew up and had his first child that we have the first record of worship. This doesn't necessarily mean that no one had expressed gratitude to God prior. It's just that humanity as a whole began to *collectively* or *corporately* call on the Lord God at this point. Genesis 4:26 tells us, "When Seth grew up, he had a son and named him Enosh. At that time people *first* began to worship the LORD by name (emphasis added)."

By Genesis 6, the effects of sin had deepened in the human race so severely that God was literally disgusted with their wickedness. Without going into too much detail, God found one man who was righteous in all the earth. Noah was his name. He had this man and his three sons build an enormous boat (ark) to preserve their family[117] and the animal kingdom when He would finally bring a worldwide flood. The purpose of this world-engulfing judgment was to rid the world of the evil that humans were spreading like cancer. It is at the end of that catastrophic event that we have the *second* record of worship.

God commanded Noah and his family to leave the ark and replenish the earth. As they departed from that which God designed to preserve the lives of all the living beings on board, Noah lead the first public time of worship. Genesis 8:20 states, "Then Noah built an altar to the Lord, and there he sacrificed as burnt offerings the animals and birds that had been approved for that purpose." Though we cannot be completely certain, it seems safe to assume that his whole family (the only living humans) was present. Also note the word *approved*; one may ask, by whom? The answer is clearly God. This further clarifies that their unified public worship was His design.

As we progress through Genesis, we see the idea of altars, sacrifices, and public worship develop from Abram (eventually renamed Abraham) to his son Isaac and then to Jacob and so forth.

In Exodus, the second book of the Bible, not long after the Israelites were supernaturally delivered from Egyptian slavery, Moses received the Ten Commandments from God. The Lord then began to further establish His plan for them to worship Him. He began to command the *corporate* celebration of feasts and Sabbaths as means of worship from them to Him. From Exodus chapter 23 and beyond, God gave instructions about building the tabernacle and the items of *public* worship therein.

The third book in the Bible, Leviticus, is about the people that God called to be His representatives (called priests) from the tribe of Levi. Again, the entire book contains God's detailed, specific, and clear directions as to how His leaders were to lead the rest of the nation in *corporate* worship. Without going through each book in the Old Testament one at a time, the pattern of God having a specific design and demand for organized corporate worship becomes noticeably clear and plain to the honest truth seeker. This continues throughout the entirety of the Old Testament. Further, it is recorded in many authentic historical writings and affirmed by a plethora of archaeological discoveries, as well as rabbinical teaching of that time.

The New Testament is viewed by Bible believing Christ followers as the fulfillment of the Old Testament. The first four books in the New Testaments are known as the gospels. Gospel means "good news" and they are primarily the account of the life of Jesus Christ, the Messiah. God sent His only Son to rescue humanity from the consequences and guilt of sin. Through Jesus, God extended His loving hand to sinful human beings who could never be holy enough (on their own) to connect with Him. This was, still is and will *always* be *good* news! God has gone to great lengths to bring justice for our sins (crimes, if you will) as any good judge would. Jesus stood in our place to pay for our sins. Therefore, justice was served[118] though substitutionally. In that severe act, God also extended His mercy to all who would come to Jesus by turning away from sin (known as repenting) with God's help and placing personal faith (trust) in Him alone for their salvation. Such good news!

Jesus is known as the "God-Man." He was full divinity wrapped in full humanity. His parents were both devout Jews. Therefore, we know that Jesus' life revolved around the temple, the Old Testament scriptures and the local synagogue.[119] It is plain then that Jesus Himself was intricately involved in public, organized, corporate worship. Since all of that was clearly a detailed part of Jewish life, and Jesus' parents were devout Jews, this seems rather obvious. This means He grew up partaking in all the Jewish feasts of corporate worship. Of course, following Jesus means primarily to do what He did— to imitate His life and teachings, to walk "in His steps."[120]

The gospel writers were Matthew, Mark, Luke, and John. Matthew and John were two of the original twelve apostles.[121] Mark interviewed many of the early followers and eyewitnesses of Jesus' life, teachings, and ministry as did Luke.

In Luke's gospel[122] chapter 3, verse 23, the good doctor tells us that "Jesus was about thirty years old when He began His public ministry." So we know that for the first three decades of His life, He was involved in the public religious community of Israel's worship. In the roughly three and one-half years of His public ministry, we can observe Jesus' involvement in the synagogue many times, in attendance at the annual feasts consistently, and participating in many of their traditions (like the Passover in Matthew 26:17–20). Though many of His own people rejected Him and He battled the religious leaders, this does not change the fact that Jesus was very involved in Israel's public, corporate, organized worship system. Remember, all of that was designed by His Father.

What follows the gospels is a book known as Acts. Other names that have been suggested explain what it is about. As mentioned in a previous chapter, those names are The Acts of the Apostles or The Acts of the Holy Spirit. This primarily records the development of what we now know as the "church." One does not have to read very far into the twenty-eight chapters of this book to discover the structure that developed under the direction of the Holy Spirit. In fact, we see it in the very first chapter! Within the context of the developing structure, the continued Judeo-Christian theme of *corporate* worship emerges once again.

Luke tells us about some final directions Jesus gave to the apostles. It states,

> Once when He was eating with them, He commanded them, "Do not leave Jerusalem until the Father sends you the gift He promised, as I told you before. John baptized with [or in] water, but in just a few days you will be baptized with [or in] the Holy Spirit."[123]

Notice that Jesus gave no indication that they had to be *together* to receive this promise. Yet we do not see them simply going back to their homes in Jerusalem (if, in fact, each one had a home there), staying in an inn alone or even meeting in clusters of small groups. Immediately thereafter, He ascended back to His Father in heaven, leaving the mission that He began to redeem fallen humanity in their hands. Where do we find them? Having encountered Jesus and His supernatural ministry for three and a half years, plus having no clear command to actually be *together* in Jerusalem, did they do what the highly individualistic western folks might do? Go off and enjoy their personal relationship with the Lord alone? Not quite!

Acts chapter 1 records,

> Then the apostles returned to Jerusalem from the Mount of Olives, a distance of half a mile. When *they* arrived, *they* went to the upstairs room of the house where *they* were staying. Here are the names of those who were present: Peter, John, James, Andrew, Philip, Thomas, Bartholomew, Matthew, James (son of Alphaeus), Simon (the Zealot), and Judas (son of James). They *all* met *together* and were constantly *united* in prayer, along with Mary the mother of Jesus, several other women, and the brothers of Jesus. During this time, when *about 120 believers were together in one place,* Peter stood up and addressed them [emphasis added]."

Peter then leads this congregation back to God's written word instructing them that the Old Testament foretold about the treachery of Judas and that his apostolic office needed to be filled. Verses 23–26 find them literally nominating two men praying together and casting lots (an Old Testament process to discover the divine will) to fill his office with Matthias. We see more structure developing.

By the end of Acts chapter 2, after the Holy Spirit came in power upon the 120 believers, we see the community of Christ followers develop even further *together*. That is the key here, which is very hard to miss—*together*. Luke writes,

> *All* the believers devoted themselves to the apostles' teaching, and to fellowship, and to *sharing* in meals (including the Lord's Supper), and to prayer. A deep sense of awe came over them all, and the apostles performed many miraculous signs and wonders. And *all* the believers met *together* in *one* place and shared everything they had. They sold their property and possessions and *shared* the money with those in need. They worshiped *together* at the Temple *each day*. (emphasis added).

Paul wrote several letters to the believers in the ancient city of Corinth of which we have two. In 1 Corinthians 11, he was addressing structure in public worship and then trying to bring order to the ordinance of communion (or the Lord's Supper). The early believers would share a meal together as an extension of their corporate worship, and the Lord's Supper was part of that. In other words, it was much more than the small elements of crackers, bread or wafer we now use in our churches. Frankly, the people of Corinth were known for their carnal ways. Well, some of them would go to these meals (*love feasts*[124]) to gorge themselves on the bread and get drunk! In 1 Corinthians 11:22, Paul says "What? Don't you have your own *homes* for eating and drinking? Or do you really want to disgrace God's *church*?" Of course, this is speaking of the public gathering of His people. The scriptures here make a distinction between any worship at home and worship in the corporate assembly.

He goes on in verse 34 and says, "If you are really hungry, eat at *home* so you won't bring judgment upon yourselves *when* [not "if"] you meet *together*" [emphasis added]. Again, this is speaking of the corporate body of Christ gathered together in worship and fellowship.

In chapters twelve to fourteen of this letter to the Corinthians, Paul was trying to bring order to the spiritual gifts, which operated in their time of worship together. In verses 19 and 28, he clarifies that he is referring to when they meet together "in church" or in "church meetings."[125] Then in verse 33, he again specifies his instructions are for "all the churches." These are obvious references to gatherings of local believers or congregations. If not, then what is he speaking of? Why are these so plainly directed to groups rather than individuals if God's intent was for each individual's worship to be expressed alone?

The purview of this book is not to do an exhaustive study of the Bible concerning whether the God who inspired these writings desires His people to worship Him both privately and publicly. However, the entire Bible contains plain teaching that God's intention is for His people to worship Him in *both* settings.[126] As stated earlier, this is not "either/or" but a "both/and" matter.

From the first book in the Bible (Genesis) to the last (Revelation), any honest study of Scripture reveals that, while His people *can* and *should* worship him privately anywhere at any time, He also wants us to worship Him in a community of likeminded believers *together*. To deny that is to deny the plain teaching of the Bible.

ARE THERE TWO CLASSES OF BELIEVERS?

Let me explain what I mean by this question. The implication by the idea that some Christ followers[127] do not need to be committed (or even involved) in a local church while others do is that there are at least two groups of believers whom God approves of. Or that God provides the church for *some* but not necessarily for *all* believers. Does the Bible indicate that it is okay for some followers of Christ to be unconnected to a local congregation while others are to be connected? Is the church only for those who feel they need that but unnecessary for those who feel they do not? Again, it seems plain that the criterion for answering this question cannot be human emotion, popular opinion or the teaching of any Christian celebrity. You guessed it. The primary question for the Christ follower is, what does the Bible say?

Following Jesus in the early days of Christendom was no pursuit for the uncommitted or faint of heart. Both Christ-followers and Jewish people were looked down upon in the Roman-Greco pagan world. Because the Romans and Greeks believed in a multitude of gods, Christians and Jews were often considered atheists because of their monotheistic view (the belief in one God). Committing to this crucified, controversial prophet who many felt was somewhat of a mystic magician who had denounced the Jewish God (or so they thought) would be like social suicide. Many paid a high price economically and relationally. It could be very discouraging.

Hebrews is a New Testament book written with many parallels to the Jewish system of worship contained in the Old Testament. In the tenth chapter, the writer tries to encourage Jesus' followers to persevere and be strong. Of course, the place they would receive the most encouragement, inspiration, and support to do that would be within the context of a group of committed believers. Sounds like a church to me!

Consider what the author writes under the Spirit's inspiration in chapter 10: "Let us think of ways to motivate one another to acts of love and good works." Being mistreated or persecuted by those who disapproved could discourage anyone from doing acts of love and good works. Remember, the people in the Bible were just that—people. They were fallen human beings. I know that many paintings and other art forms make them appear as super-holy people whose heads are wrapped in halos, but I assure you, that is simply not accurate. In fact, Jesus' half-brother, James, gives us some insight into this about one of the most well-respected and powerful Hebrew prophets—Elijah. This guy was amazing.

He did all kinds of supernatural acts involving both the human body and nature itself. He prayed and announced that there would be no rain in the land until he said so, which was three and half years.[128] He made gallons and gallons of oil and flour come from a couple of small containers for a poor widow during a famine (which the lack of rain brought) so that her and her son could eat many days.[129] When that widow's son died suddenly, he raised the young boy from the dead.[130] On two separate occasions, he commanded fire to come down from heaven, and it consumed fifty soldiers each time.[131] I could list many more things the Bible shows of his supernatural feats. If any guy in the Bible had a halo, it must have been him, right?

Okay, onto what James[132] wrote about this godly man called Elijah in the fifth chapter of his letter.

> Elijah was *as human as we are* [emphasis added], and yet when he prayed earnestly that no rain would fall, none fell for three and a half years! Then, when he prayed again, the sky sent down rain and the earth began to yield its crops.

The point is, what the writer of Hebrews wrote in chapter 10 verse 24 was because even the *strongest* of God's people can get discouraged. Persecution and stress was wearing them down. This could motivate them to give up trying to follow Jesus in order to regain all they had forfeited. They could easily become bitter and unloving toward others and stop living out their faith in love and kind deeds. So the writer encourages them to "think of ways to motivate *one another* [emphasis added] to love and good works."

There are many instructions to the New Testament believer that involve the words *one another*. Those directives were written by a Spirit-inspired Christ follower to other Christ followers. Well, you cannot "one another" unless you are actually *with* "one another"! Please note that there is no distinction indicating that this was only for some and not for others. In order for the mission of Jesus to continue and be effective, they *had* to stick together like glue to encourage and support one another. It is critical to understand the ultimate mission of the church is far more than personal fulfillment. It is not for our entertainment and, as is so popular these days, to get our needs met. That is a self-centered religion at best! The followers of Christ have far more to consider. Church is not about us. It is about Him and how He reaches through us to gather as many into the ark of safety before the time of judgment.

> The writer of Hebrews continues, "And let us not neglect our meeting together, *as some people do* [emphasis added], but encourage one another, especially now that the day of his return is drawing near."

So evidently, there *were* two groups of followers! He addresses both. Clearly, some people *were* neglecting meeting together while others were not. Those in neglect had other things replacing that fellowship. This passage instructs them not to continue in that pattern. The Spirit admonishes them to come into alignment with His plan and *one another* again!

Further, he says, "Especially now that the day of His return is drawing near."[133] Consider the way another translation words this passage: "And let us consider how we may spur one another on toward love and good deeds, *not giving up meeting together*, as *some* are in the *habit* of doing, but encouraging one another—*and all the more as you see the Day approaching*."[134] (emphasis added) Remember, this was written nearly two millennia ago. The day of His return is *much* nearer now than it was then! So the issue of some giving up meeting together is really nothing new. But the admonishment has not changed.

Not realizing the many passages and principles that direct followers to be part of a corporate body, one man referred to the aforementioned Hebrews passage and said, "The Bible only says we have to be part of the church once." Even if that were true, which it is not, how many times does God have to command something for a professing follower until he or she obeys? If God is truly one's god, I would think just once is enough!

The apostle Paul wrote most of the New Testament. In his letter to the Christ followers in Rome, referring to the corporate church, he wrote in chapter 12, "We are many parts *of one body*, and we all *belong* to each other [emphasis added]." That word *belong* really rubs against our rebellious nature, does it not? And yet, it is very clear. How can Christ followers *belong* to each other and yet remain separate? The illustration that Paul is giving in this section parallels the members of the human body (arms, legs, fingers, etc.) with the body (congregation) of Christ followers. Like the members of the human body are all connected, supportive of one another, and moving *together* (there's that word again), so it is with the church. It is just as unnatural for the members of the body of Christ to attempt to operate alone as it would be for the members of a human body to! Imagine that! That is the picture the Holy Spirit has drawn through these writings of Paul.

In the light of scripture, a churchless Christian is not only an oxymoron but is also like a disconnected body part! To take

Paul's analogy more fully, can a body part be attached to the head and not to the other members? Perhaps an ear or nose, but even those parts actually on the head still work together with the other members under the direction of the head for the good of the *entire* body, not just the member itself. In the words of John Wesley, the founder of the Methodist church, "The Bible knows nothing of solitary religion."[135]

In light of all that, to answer the question, "Are there two different classes (or groups) of believer?" The answer is no. What God has instructed for one follower of Jesus, in terms of their connection and commitment to the corporate body, He instructs to all the rest. To think that one can be connected to the head of the body (that is Jesus in this case) and yet not be to the members seems not only preposterous but downright prideful and arrogant.

* * *

"Special-privilege parkers." That is what my family and I call those people who like to park places where the signs tell them they cannot. You know, they pull up right in front of Walmart, parking in the fire lane with the vehicle running, hindering traffic and blocking customers but somehow it's okay because they are not technically parked. (Really? What gear are they in?) Or how about those who park in the handicapped spots when they are not handicapped? But somehow it's okay because they are just running in quickly. For whatever reason, some people seem to think that rules or principles do not apply to them, implying that they are somehow special. The implication is that they are in a different class of people with special privileges. Arrogant, don't you think? Isn't the spiritual parallel obvious?

* * *

IS CHRISTIAN MEDIA REALLY
"FELLOWSHIP"?

To one repetitive kid I said, "You sound like a broken record."

He said, "What's a 'record'?" Good grief. I grew up with turn tables, and we thought we reached the improvement zenith when the eight-track came out! With the advent of digital files, iTunes, mp3s, and the iPhone, even CD players are old-school now. I remember when cassettes came out, and we thought technology could hardly get more efficient. Dolby noise reduction? What's that? Most people born after 1980 probably have no idea unless they saw it in their parent's car.

Are you old enough to remember the Atari table-tennis game? I am laughing as I type this remembering sitting in front of a black-and-white screen and turning that archaic joystick as the little dot traveled at what now seems like the speed of a mentally-challenged snail on barbiturates. My kids try to get me to play the Wii, PS3, or the X-Box 360. The speed of the characters alone make my head spin! Yet I watch teenagers play it like it was so simple. They would probably laugh till they could not any longer if they ever saw the Atari games that were so cool to us back in the day...*way* back.

What a day we live in. With the electronic age has come all kinds of communicatory improvements. Cable TV—what once seemed so incredible back in the eighties—now seems like something dated back to the time of the Flintstones. VCRs were replaced with DVD players, which are now being upstaged with Blu-ray, satellite, HDTV, plasma TV, the Internet, live streaming, Hulu, Netflix, YouTube, Facebook, Twitter, Pinterest, Tumblr, Reddit, blogs, Skype, Sirius Satellite Radio, podcasts, iPods, iPhones, iPads, Androids, eBooks, apps, GPS, eBay, Craigslist, Amazon.com, who can even keep up?

With all those technological advancements has come a plethora of ways for messages to be communicated. Of course, this is a great thing. It has brought nearly unlimited opportunities to advance the message of Christ. In my opinion, that has good points and "not so good" points. The fact that the good news of God's forgiveness and grace can be broadcasted in so many ways into so many places is astonishing and grounds for great rejoicing for Christ followers.

*   *   *

As I mentioned earlier,[136] I came to Christ in 1981 when I was twenty-one years old. My religious background provided me no clue about what a "fellowship" meant or truly is. So when our church single's group leader announced they were having one at her house, I was left to try to figure out what it even was. When you are new to the whole church thing, some of the lingo, acrostics, and jargon can really confuse you. It sounds like coded language for club members only.

Well, I have discovered that some church people call any time they spend together "fellowship." I guess they feel a need to have a spiritual word for every activity, or else maybe it is somehow unholy or displeasing to God. A bunch of people are going out for pizza, they call it "fellowship." Two friends are going to work out together at the gym, it's "fellowship." Many have seemed to exchange this word for *any* interaction between two or more Christ followers. Respectfully, it is important to understand what the believer is encouraged to be a part of in this all-important word. Christ followers are share their very lives together!

It seems wise to explain then what the word *fellowship* means in a Christian context. The Greek word for fellowship is *koinonia*, and it speaks of a close relational connection. It really speaks of community and joint participation, as well as sharing in the benefits of that union.[137]

In the Christian context, this would certainly be Christ centered. It is the sharing of things revolving around Christ. It's sharing life together and building a strong relational and supportive connection between believers. This is a group of people who live their lives in close relational proximity not primarily for their own fulfillment and pleasure but for what is best for everyone in that faith-community in the long run. For Christ followers, a community of believers does all they can for the common good of God's people and mission in accordance with the Bible and the guidance of the Holy Spirit. This is what the first followers of Christ were devoted to[138] and such is the plain intention of God for His people throughout time and eternity.

Back to what I said a couple of paragraphs ago, media to advance the message of the gospel is good, *if* it is viewed and used properly in light of what the God of the Bible has called his people to—community. The church *is* a community, a group of committed followers of Jesus Christ doing their utmost to live out their master's teachings and to imitate his life (albeit quite imperfectly). This requires relationships, the communication and sharing of thoughts, insights, burdens, fears, dreams, etc. Community is about sharing mutual support and encouragement. The key words there are *sharing* and *mutual*. Does listening to Christian radio, TV, CDs, podcasts, or the like provide anything that involves two parties (or more) sharing anything *mutually*? Not usually. In fact, very rarely, if at all.

Studies vary in the numbers, but communication is about 7 percent in the actual words and 93 percent in body language, facial expression, and voice intonation. The breakdown of that 93 percent shows that even talking by phone (whether cell, landline, or smart phone) reduces communication to less than 40 percent of its best expression.[139] When people are not face-to-face, any supposed mutual sharing is minimal at best.

This word *fellowship* is rather revealing. God directs us into it because it is His very nature. A study of the nature of God (theology) reveals that He is outside of time. Did you ever wonder what God was doing before He created time and space? Okay, this may get a little deep.

The Bible shows that God is a being of plurality. When God was considering creating humans He said, "Let *Us* make human beings in *Our* image, to be like *Us*."[140] (emphasis added) Did you catch that? Who is *Us*? God created everything so, who is He talking to? It could not be the angels because He did not create humans in their image. Neither could it have been another deity as He did not create them in anyone else's image but His own.[141] He is speaking to the other members of the triune God or what some of refer to as the trinity. The very first sentence in the Bible states emphatically, "In the beginning God created the heavens and the earth."[142] As we read more scripture, we discover that the word *God* refers to more than one person who existed and was present.

In John's gospel, we are told that there was a second person there as well. The apostle writes, "In the beginning the Word already existed. The Word was with God, *and the Word was God.*"[143] (emphasis added) In that same chapter, verse 14 tells us that "the Word became human and made His home among us. He was full of unfailing love and faithfulness. And we have seen His glory, the glory of the Father's *one and only Son.*" (emphasis added) Of course, this refers to Jesus, the Son of God. We see Jesus claim to be God multiple times in the New Testament.[144] The writers of the New Testament affirm this over and over.

More study of the Bible reveals that there was even a third Person there as well. Before anything or anyone was created, the Bible says "The *Spirit* of God [emphasis added] was hovering over the surface of the waters."[145] He too is referred to as God on many occasions.[146]

Now this gets a bit confusing when we see God asserting that he is the one and only being who preexisted before time and space.[147] Thus we see that the God of the Bible is one God existent in three persons, all of which are equally God. Each has their role that the other two do not. They work together, supporting each other. At this point, you may be thinking, "Thanks for the theology lesson but what in the world has any of this got to do with the question?"

The Bible declares that "God is love."[148] *Love needs an object.* It does not and cannot exist independently. God could not be "love" if He were a singular Being. His very *nature* is a community; a *fellowship*. He directs His followers to be like Him in a variety of ways. We are to "be holy in everything [we] do" because He is holy.[149] We are to "be imitators of God, as beloved children. And walk in love, as Christ loved us and gave Himself up for us."[150] We are also to be like Him in fellowship; a community of mutually supportive and caring people reflecting the nature of God.

When we look at the lives of the Jewish community in the Old Testament, the earthly life of Jesus and that of the early church, we see people living life together, closely, mutually, and consistently in community. This is true fellowship. The apostle John gives some great insight as to the results of those who live in fellowship with Jesus Christ. He writes, "But if we are living in the light, as God is in the light, then we have fellowship with each other, and the blood of Jesus, His Son, cleanses us from all sin."[151] Thus those who are in close relationship with Jesus, will also desire and live in fellowship with each other. The result will be that the blood of Jesus will cleanse them from all sin. Now I am not trying to be people's judge. That is God's job, but could this be the reason why so many people who claim to believe in God are so entangled in a variety of harmful patterns of life, i.e., not cleansed but polluted instead?

Many professing Christians have exchanged the community of believers in a local congregation for "feeding" themselves at home or wherever they see fit. As a pastor, I do not even know how many times I have heard people who drift away in their church attendance say, "But I'm reading my Bible and praying at home." Or "I watch (insert the most popular TV preacher's name here) at home," as if that is what God has required. As if following Jesus is reduced to their own pursuit of God in a self-controlled environment, completely under their own terms—no sharing of life, no giving of themselves in ministry efforts to help others, no mutual support of any kind.

When Christian media is used as a *supplement* to a strong, committed, dedicated life lived in community and fellowship with God's people, then and only then is it being used properly.[152] By the way, the vast majority of those heard by podcast, TV preachers, and Christian musicians, who are truly following the God of the Bible on His terms, would tell you the very same thing. I guarantee it.

Friend, if you believe in the God of the Bible, let me assure you, He has so much more for you than being a lone-ranger seeking God on your own without the benefits of guidance from a caring pastor, prayer support from loving Christians, and opportunities to advance His cause in this temporary world. Please understand, God's directives into true biblical fellowship are for your benefit, the common good of the rest of the congregation, and to attract others to Himself through His followers. I know that church is full of imperfect people. Unless you yourself are perfect, would you really want it any other way? If it were only for those who live everything they say and believe perfectly, no one could attend, including me!

On behalf of pastors, Christians and congregations everywhere, I invite you to come and enjoy true community and fellowship. God will lead you to the place where you fit best and, once you get settled and fix your focus on the perfect God instead of His imperfect people, you will absolutely love it! Imitate those godly characteristics you see in people, and when you see characteristics that do not agree with godliness, realize that we all have them and try not to imitate them. We human beings will always fall short. Isn't that why we needed a savior in the first place? Come and connect with the ordinary and fallen feeble people of the extraordinary and perfect God. That's true fellowship!

WHERE SHOULD MY FINANCIAL SUPPORT GO?

The place you live is free, right? How about your mode of transportation? Your food? Clothes? Heat? Air conditioning? Higher education? Honestly, can you name *anything* besides things like air and sunshine that are free? Of course not. So why is it that people seem to think that everything in a religious organization should be free?

I know that there have been plenty of phonies and religious charlatans over the years that have used religion and spirituality as a means to get money out of innocent people, but they are the *exceptions* by an enormous margin. The vast majority of churches and other religious organizations are sincerely trying to live out what they believe. This takes organization, equipment, staff support, supplies, and a variety of other things like rent (or a mortgage on property), advertisement, paper supplies, postage, etc. How many of those things are free? Of course, you know, none of them are. It all takes financial support and usually lots of it.

I still remember my first car. Well, it was actually my parents'. First they let my older sister drive it, and then I more or less took it over. It was a light-blue 1968 Dodge Dart with a slant 6 engine. I beat the daylights out of that poor thing.

It was considered cool to spin your tires and "burn rubber" in the high school parking lot. A slant-6 engine in the family car cannot really do too much of that. So what did this sixteen-year-old punk do? Of course, I would put it in reverse, go about 20 miles per hour, drop the gears in to first, and floor it! Man, those wheels would smoke! To this day, I do not know how I didn't drop the transmission right there on the pavement. I did this all the time.

Fast forward to my first year after high school, I bought a 1971 Ford Torino with an 8-cylinder 302 engine in it—much more power than the Dart. I put in the best sound system I could afford. I used to wash and wax it regularly. The windows were clear because I cleaned them often. In the first six months I owned it, I spent more money on it than I paid for it just to keep it running. Now with all that extra horsepower (in comparison to the Dart, I mean), you would think I smoked those tires even more than that puny little 6-cylinder, right? Wrong.

Why was it so easy to do what I did to my parents' car without concern? Besides the fact that I was a self-centered, idiotic, rebellious jerk who disrespected my parents. It was because I did not pay for it. Not one dime. The only thing I did was put gas in it and perform some basic maintenance. Because I invested nothing into it, I had little concern for it. I had no sense of ownership. However, I babied that Torino like it was a Maserati. Why? Because I invested in it. I owned it. I took personal responsibility for it, that's why.

Many people treat the church the way I treated that Dart. They want to use the church for their own pleasure and fulfillment without investing in it. Because of this self-centeredness (like me at sixteen), they have little concern for the Owner of it (though they profess they do) and His purposes for it. They abuse her, use her, and give little, if anything, to her cause. They like to *take* but not to *give*. Like my parents' car was viewed by me as existing primarily for my pleasure no matter what it cost them, some view the church in the same way and refuse to share in the cost of its mission, purpose, and upkeep.

The God of the Bible has always had ways for His work on earth to be supported, and it was always through His people. How else would it be? God gives His people the privilege and truly the honor of having ownership of His work on this planet. He wants His own to care for His church. I am not referring to the building, although that structure is to facilitate what He really cares about—ministry to *people*. The fact of the matter is, the building costs money. The seats, heating, air conditioning, sound equipment, copy machine, parking lot, and every single other thing there all costs something. From the toilet paper to the insurance, from the secretary to the postage and website, it all costs money, and lots of it!

Tithing. That may be a new, different and possibly even annoying concept to you. The word *tithe* literally means "a tenth." It's easy and fair to everyone. God has not asked the rich to give more than the less fortunate percentage wise—just a tenth. Just move the decimal over one digit, and you will not even need a calculator. If I have $10.00, then a tithe would be $1.00. Simple. This is the way that God has instructed for His earthly work to be supported, giving His people the privilege of partnership with Him. How cool is that? God does not *need* a thing from any of us but *welcomes* us to join with Him in His earthly endeavors!

It started four centuries *before* the Law of Moses (the first five books in the Bible) was instituted. Abram gave a tithe to God's representative.[153] Clearly, this became an active practice that he taught his descendants as we see his grandson Jacob doing the same thing.[154] The practice is then incorporated into the law in the Old Testament then endorsed by Jesus Christ on two separate occasions.[155] We'll consider that in a little more detail shortly.

Many church people are still debating over this issue. Whether you believe in it or not, whether you think you should tithe on your *gross* income or your *net* income, whether you think you should be able to just give an offering as you desire and determine, the Christ follower gives. No sincere believer could deny we *are* to give!

In the Sermon on the Mount in Matthew chapters five to seven, having professed Himself as the king, Jesus took these three chapters to explain the principles of His kingdom. Speaking to His followers, He said, *"When* you give," not *"If* you give"¹⁵⁶[emphasis added]. Though this passage deals with giving to the poor and is not really focused on tithing or offerings to a church per se, the principle is still the same. The Bible instructs believers in many other places to give to God's work in and through the local congregation.¹⁵⁷ This book is not about whether or not one should give to the church. It seems obvious that there is no other way for it to continue because everything costs money. Those who follow Jesus are expected to give to further His work and mission on earth, period.

The question then arises, *how* are we to do that? *Where* is the money to go? Does it even matter? Whether you agree with me or not, let me explain about tithing. When someone first told me about it, frankly, the idea of giving 10 percent of my income sounded ludicrous! Why? Primarily because I was cheap and greedy. I am a pampered American. I have never gone to bed truly hungry, never done without clothes, heat in the winter, a car in my family, or the latest electronic gadgets, but somehow, I always think I need more. I think that's the case with those of us who reside in the West.

Missions and humanitarian organizations tell us that thousands of children die from starvation or malnutrition every day, but somehow I see myself, who has three square meals a day, snacks in between, a variety of beverages to pick from and has to struggle to *lose* weight as needy. How sad and absurd! Truthfully, most of us Americans are like that—cheap, greedy, and pampered, always wanting something more.

As I mentioned earlier, the first time we see anyone give a tenth (tithe) is when Abram returning from a battle in Genesis 14. He gave it to Melchizedek the high priest (God's representative) at that time.¹⁵⁸ Though the king of Sodom, not the priest, offered to give it back, there's no record of Melchizedek doing so. Even if he had, it would not change the fact that Abram willingly gave it as an act of gratitude and worship to God. We see that this godly practice continued when we note that his grandson Jacob promised God that he would do the same thing.[159]

This practice, which I already mentioned, began more than four centuries *before* the Law of Moses, was instituted in the book of Exodus and was then explained in great detail in the rest of the law (Exodus through Deuteronomy). The Jewish people practiced it throughout their entire history. An honest study of the Old Testament shows that to be plainly true. Consider these words from the last prophet who wrote in said testament:

> "I am the Lord, and I do not change. That is why you descendants of Jacob are not already destroyed. Ever since the days of your ancestors, you have scorned my decrees and failed to obey them. Now *return to me, and I will return to you*," says the Lord of Heaven's Armies. "But you ask, '*How* can we return when we have never gone away?' "Should people cheat God? Yet you have cheated me! "But you ask, 'What do you mean? When did we ever cheat you?' "You have cheated me of the *tithes and offerings due to me*. You are under a curse, for your whole nation has been cheating me. Bring *all* the tithes into the *storehouse* so there will be enough food in my Temple. *If you do,*" *says the Lord of Heaven's Armies, "I will open the windows of heaven for you. I will pour out a blessing so great you won't have enough room to take it in! Try it! Put me to the test!* Your crops will be abundant, for I will guard them from insects and disease. Your grapes will not fall from the vine before they are ripe," says the Lord of Heaven's Armies."[160] [emphasis added.]

Without going into great detail about this passage, let's just consider the following. The people had come to disobey the Lord, and He called them to return to Him. They were not sure *how*, and He clarified that they had turned away from Him by *cheating* Him of the tithes and offerings *due* Him (when giving to God's work, we are in essence giving to *Him*). The fruitless and spiritually dry climate they were in was a direct result of their stinginess toward the person and work of God.

Further, consider that He instructs them to bring *all* the tithes, not just *some*, but a full 10 percent into the storehouse. The storehouses were rooms in the outer perimeter of the temple. Why should they do this? So there will be enough food in His temple. This refers to supplies for the business of the temple and to the support of the priests. This support fed them and allowed them to focus on their calling—ministry to God's people at His place of choice, the temple.

Lastly, please note the promise that comes to those who obey. This is the only area a believer is actually *invited* and encouraged to put God *to the test*. He promises that those who obey will receive far more than they give and plenty for their own needs. He does more with the 90 percent He allows His people to keep than we could ever do with the 100 percent. I have lived this out for three decades and found it to be true.

When we come to the New Testament, primarily the life of Christ and the teaching of His chosen apostles, we do not see it mentioned much. Why? First of all, when something has been practiced repeatedly for hundreds and thousands of years, does there still need to be a strong emphasis on it? Isn't it clear by that point?

But also, we must remember that a big part of why Jesus came was to *raise the standard* of God's people. Instead of His followers simply trying to cooperate with a law externally, He calls and equips His own to live godly in the heart, where no one can see. The entire Sermon on the Mount is about that. In Matthew 5, he said, "Don't misunderstand why I have come. I did not come to abolish the Law of Moses or the writings of the prophets. No, I came to accomplish their purpose." Further, on two separate occasions, Jesus said to those wanting to follow the God of the Bible, "You should tithe."[161] Also, since Jesus came to *raise* the standard, if a tithe was the requirement before and during the law, that would seem to be the *starting* point in the New Covenant, don't you think?

So in light of all that, several issues arise that pertains to the thrust of this book. If we are going to go by the Bible, in order to serve the God who inspired it, one must give from their means to partner with Him and His people so His work here is supported. Giving to the poor and to charities is Christlike and part of following Jesus,[162] but that is not necessarily supporting the work of His *gospel* through the public witness of the church in particular locales that He has ordained.

The same Bible that offers us grace, forgiveness, salvation, answered prayer, etc., also says we are to tithe. It also says *where* the tithe is supposed to go—the *storehouse*. During the First Covenant, that would be the Temple. In the Second Covenant, the place where God's work is carried out the clearest and the most effective is the local church, not a TV preacher nor a Christian ministry of any kind.

As useful and wonderful as para-church ministries can be, do they walk with you day to day so you can both encourage each other through the ups and downs in life? Do they mobilize you to bring Christ to those around you so that if and when they come to faith they can then be mentored into following Jesus? Do they establish true biblical fellowship with you and your family? Do they provide age-appropriate ministry for your children teaching them line upon line how to follow Christ? Can you call them when you're in crisis and have someone come out to be with you? No. It is the local church that typically provides all of that. It is the local church that is the God-ordained *storehouse*.

So then, someone who professes to want to follow the God of the Bible yet has little or nothing to do with a local church has no *biblical* way to support His work with their finances. I don't mean to be harsh, but that only leaves one option—disobedience. Please understand, *partial* obedience is *disobedience*. Basically, to

CHURCH! WHO NEEDS IT?!

follow the God of the Bible those are the two options: obey what He has instructed in His Word, or disobey. Yes, it's really *that* plain and simple. So are you treating the church like I treated my '68 Dodge Dart or like I treated that '71 Ford Torino?

WHY HAVE THE GIFTS AND CALLINGS?

God has given gifts to every single person. Many of these are natural. By that, I mean that He worked them into the fabric of who each person is, whether they follow His Son or not. However, it's crystal clear from Scripture that He has also distributed *spiritual* gifts to each and every follower of his Son Jesus Christ. Though in one sense, God has a calling on every person to do and be something for Him, there are also those whom God has called to specific offices in the Body of Christ.

Paul the Apostle was one such man. He writes in his letter to the church at Ephesus in chapter 4:

> So Christ Himself gave the apostles, the prophets, the evangelists, the pastors and teachers, to equip His people for works of service, so that the body of Christ may be built up until we all reach unity in the faith and in the knowledge of the Son of God and become mature, attaining to the whole measure of the fullness of Christ.[163]

Since the responsibility of equipping God's people for works of service for all the purposes that follow verse 11 in the above passage do not end till Christ returns, it only stands to reason that those offices will be needed until then as well. While there may be some disagreement among God's people as to just how that plays out, there is *not* any debate that He has indeed given gifts and callings to whomever He desired to. You may ask, "What has that got to do with the discussion at hand?"

We need only consider, what are the *purposes* for these gifts? Verse 12 says, "To equip *His people*." [emphasis added] Well, who is that? The church. It is His called-out ones who have placed personal faith in Jesus the Christ. These are each *organizational* gifts meant for an *organized* movement, an *organization*. You guessed it, the church. One has to then only ask, if followers of Jesus do not really need to be part of the organized church, why would He do that? Those in these God-ordained offices serve as mentors with authority who bring a great sense of accountability, thus helping to guide the public witness and impact of Christ followers. This is all to further the mission Jesus began and then gave His followers when He ascended. That is to *"go and make disciples."*[164] (emphasis added)

What follows is in no way an exhaustive or comprehensive definition of each of the aforementioned callings but rather a general explanation to make the point.

Apostles. Jesus picked the first twelve[165] and then others were added.[166] A modern-day apostle is someone called to start churches, raise up leaders from within those churches and plant more. He then oversees them in this multiplication process so the spread of the gospel continues. It seems prudent to mention that they do not carry the same level of authority as the original twelve did.

Prophets. They speak for God, period. They foretell events or information that is in the future. They also know and share information for the present revealed to them by God that they could not know otherwise. In the New Testament era, they primarily operate within the congregational setting.[167] As with the apostolic gift, today's prophet does not carry the same level of authority the Old Testament prophets did as we now have the full canon of Scripture.[168]

Evangelists. Philip is the only scriptural example we have of one.[169] He was someone who served in a local church as a deacon, traveled to preach the gospel to the unconverted, and was used mightily in supernatural gifts. His giftedness more than likely inspired others to share their faith more boldly, and he would then have had instructed them in that way. No doubt, he kept himself accountable to the elders and apostles who served over him.

Pastors. It comes from a Latin word, which refers to a shepherd and feeder of sheep.[170] As a shepherd would watch over a flock to protect, care for, feed, lead, and breed them, so a pastor does with the people of his congregation. He is their loving and committed spiritual leader.

Teachers. Someone who has studied the Word of God and explains what it meant in its original context, what it means for those to whom he is speaking, and then how to apply it practically in their life.

Let's also consider what the Apostle Paul refers to as "the gifts of the Spirit" in 1 Corinthians 12:1. The abuse and misuse of them was a major problem in the church at Corinth. This is why he spent three entire chapters (almost 20 percent of his letter) to discuss them. Before we take another brief cursory look at them, understand that he states in no uncertain terms that they are for the "common good,"[171] or, as the New Living Translation puts it, "to help *each other.*" (emphasis added) Keeping in mind he is writing to an organized group of Christ followers, may I state the obvious? Once again, it becomes clear that the gifts that follow are to operate primarily (though not exclusively) within the context of a congregation. Each one comes through a Christ follower and primarily functions with a gathering of believers where there is accountability and godly authority (we'll discuss those in the next question). Let's look at them briefly.

Wisdom. This consists of a message from God granting His point of view of one's situation and thus His counsel. It is typically given to an individual but is also given to a congregation through a believer to confirm God's direction.

Knowledge. This is information that the speaker does not know and could not have known through natural human means.

Through it the recipient often gains insight about how to resolve a problem or issue.

Faith. Though God gives a "measure of faith" to each believer,[172] this is a greater level for a specific thing He wants to do through that person. It is an absolute unshakeable certainty about an act of God that is forthcoming.

Gifts of healing. Through the blood of his dear Son, God has provided for our *spiritual* healing, which opens the possibility for *physical* healing.[173] The Holy Spirit often heals someone's body, mind, emotions, memories, etc. through a Christ follower as they pray for the sick.

Miraculous powers. A miracle is when God interrupts what would be the natural order and flow of something. For instance, if God redirects a tornado so that it does not destroy something that was clearly in its path, that would be a miracle. Of course, a multitude of examples could be given.

Prophecy. Prophetic utterances can be *forth*telling—truths that cut through the unnecessary or what may be surface issues and exposes the heart of a matter. They can also be *fore*telling, revealing things that are yet to be.

Discernment of spirits. The one with this gift becomes keenly aware of the source of something supposedly from God. The enemies of our souls (the devil and the fallen angels) are masters of deception. In fact, the Apostle Paul said he "masquerades as an angel of light,"[174] meaning an angel of God. This gift is very helpful in keeping the followers of Jesus from being deceived.

Tongues. This is when someone speaks out above the average volume of the congregation in a language they have never studied or known. It can be a message for someone in that congregation who speaks that exact language. However, since 1 Corinthians 14:2 says the "One who speaks in a tongue speaks *not* to men *but to God,*" (emphasis added) it should reflect words of praise and adoration for Him more often than not.

Interpretation of tongues. Without this gift, only the speaker of tongues benefits,[175] not the congregation. This was a major issue in Corinth for the people were trying to outdo each other (believe it or not) by everyone speaking loudly in their Spirit-inspired unknown language, and it was bringing confusion to nonfollowers who had happened into their public worship times.

While there are more gifts mentioned in the Bible, considering these alone is pertinent to the question at hand. What is obvious about all of these is that though God can inspire them in public, they operate primarily within an organized group of Christ followers, a local congregation. Let me restate an earlier question. Why in the world would God design such gifts and callings to operate among His people in an organized way if the church is simply an invention of human beings? Or if Christ followers don't really need it, or as it has been suggested, some need it while others do not? Isn't the answer rather plain?

WHAT ABOUT AUTHORITY AND ACCOUNTABILITY?

These are two issues those of us in the Western world, particularly my fellow Americans, really wrestle with. More accurately, we bristle and resist both. I am convinced that they are at the very *core* of the issue that runs through this book.

Before we consider these things further as they relate to the church, it is critical to understand that all authority in this world is delegated. Every person's authority can be traced back to another person, an organization, an agreement (contract, covenant, etc.) or all three. However, tracing authority all the way to where it originates brings us back to God. He is the ultimate authority. In His Spirit-inspired letter to the Christ followers in Rome, who, by the way, were under the cruel dominion of a Roman dictator who enjoyed torturing God's people, Paul the Apostle wrote, "All authority comes from God, and those in positions of authority have been placed there by God."[176] I know this leaves us with some questions, especially the second half of the verse. Nonetheless, it is true. As I keep saying, take *all* of the Bible or take *none* of it. It does not make sense any other way.

Applied to the body of Christ (His church), one must recognize every teacher, pastor, elder, and leader has been placed there by God. Recognizing and accepting this fact leads one to benefit from that authority as God intended. To resist this truth causes one to miss all the blessing God planned, even from those leaders who are not all they should be, provided they are not abusive. We may choose to say that God simply *allowed* a leader to be there whom we either do not approve of or who eventually failed. However, since He is all-powerful, He also could have *prevented* it, yet He did not. A bit of a theological conundrum, I know. Yet the scripture we just looked at is clear: *those* in positions of authority, not just the position or office itself, as some suggest, have been placed there by God.

Further, every human being will give an account of themselves to Him one day. Jesus' friend Matthew recorded something He said in chapter 16 of his gospel, "For the Son of Man [a messianic term referring to Himself] will come with His angels in the glory of His Father and will judge *all* [emphasis added] people according to their deeds." Understand, this is one of many scriptures that plainly tell us that each and every human being with the ability to understand and respond to the truth will one day answer to Him for all they have done.

One other statement Jesus made really emphasizes the depth of this in a sobering manner. I encourage you read these words from Matthew chapter 12 slowly and digest the plain meaning of them:

> Out of the abundance of the heart the mouth speaks. The good person out of his good treasure brings forth good, and the evil person out of his evil treasure brings forth evil.

I tell you, on the day of judgment people will give account *for every careless word they speak* [emphasis added], for by your words you will be justified, and by your words you will be condemned.

Why? Because the words reveal what's in the *heart* as verse 34 states. As one man said, "The tongue is a tattletale and it tells on the heart."[177]

The point of these previous paragraphs in this section is this: God has designed authority to *help* us not *hurt* us and accountability aids people in staying on His path. If responded to properly, except in rare isolated situations, authority and accountability will bring direction, peace of mind, and stability. However, our sinful nature resists both. We make our own assessments of people, consider the errors of leaders, look to America's founding fathers and other mortal measuring tools to determine if we are going to "submit to governing authorities."[178] Therein is one of the primary causes of the anemia we see so prevalent in the church.

Frankly, unless one is being asked to violate what God says, He does not bless rebellion against authority no matter how spiritual one can make it seem.[179] With His blessing removed, the person(s) is left to the influences of culture, what's popular (amongst professing Christians and non) or just their own carnal intellect to determine what is best. Do you see how the absence of God's touch, as well as those other avenues, would lead to a fragmented, weak, and ineffective church unable to impact their society as God intended?

Resistance to authority and avoidance of accountability make a person an island unto himself. Such a one cannot be reached with the highest quality of resources God wanted to send. Also, this pattern leaves them unprepared for eternity when they will face the source of all authority and be held accountable for their lives.

A popular bumper sticker reads, Question Authority. There is certainly a time and place to do that; however, if that's a general principle of one's daily life, the heart of the matter is the matter in the heart—rebellion. Underneath all the rhetoric or even spiritual-sounding arguments is simply a heart that wants to rule. It reveals someone who sees themselves as the final authority. It is one who does not want anyone questioning them, so they reflect the questioning back at the questioner. Deep inside, one who lives this way would not want the same philosophy of life projected onto them. You may wonder how I know. When was the last time you saw a parent put the words *Question Authority* on an article of clothing for their own child? Why don't they? The answer is simple. They don't want *their* authority challenged—can I say it—revealing their hypocrisy.

Authority and accountability are like Siamese twins. They depend on, build up, feed, and respect each other. Only one who recognizes and willingly submits to authority benefits from accountability. A person who embraces accountability recognizes their own shortcomings and inability to know all things, thus admitting that they are not the final authority. This person is free to mature and develop in the things of God and typically becomes even more tender-hearted and Christlike. That being said, whether it seems to work or not isn't the primary issue for the Christ follower; rather, it is obedience to the Word of God and, therefore, the God of the Word.

The professing follower of Christ who feels he or she does not need to be committed to the church and submitted to her leaders typically becomes less and less teachable, more and more argumentative, and ultimately ends up reflecting the very thing they thought they were avoiding—an angry, unloving, bitter, and hypocritical Christian. They attain all that without the church no less!

To those professing believers who feel they do not and will not be part of the church, please consider who is holding you accountable? What authority of the leaders that God has put in position are you submitted to? Anyone with any history in the church world would agree that there are enough poor examples of godly leaders to go around, but that's not the question, if you genuinely want to follow the God of the Bible, is it? Let God deal with His "less than perfect" leaders—the same gracious God who wants to deal with you when you mess up. If you really want to be like Christ, offer grace as He did from the cross when He prayed for His malicious murderers. "Father, forgive them, for they don't know [truly understand] what they are doing."[180] Pray for them. Support them. Encourage them.

Also, seek God for friends who want to follow Christ and are a part of a healthy church. Walk together with them and lovingly hold each other accountable. All of that will help you live a life pleasing to God, experience His peace and blessing, plus prepare you for the day when you will see Him because you will!

ARE INDEPENDENT CHRISTIANS EFFECTIVE?

By independent, I mean someone professing to follow Jesus Christ as He is defined in the orthodoxy of scripture but not attending a local church, which teaches those very scriptures— i.e., one who would say, "I'm following Jesus *my* way, and I don't really *have* to be part of a church to do that."

As an American, I love the Fourth of July. It represents the day that our nation was formed apart from the tyranny of King George and Great Britain. It is the day we declared our independence from them. While that was clearly divine providence and a wonderful thing, the rugged individualism that was thus spawned into our ideological DNA is not always so good. The idea of and commitment to a community is often filtered through a certain level of self-centeredness.

The New Testament refers to the church as a bride, a body, and a building. Note how each illustration involves *inter*dependency.

In a healthy marriage, it takes a groom and a *bride* working together to have a good and happy life. The human *body* is made up of many parts and functions best when each member of it submits to the head and does its part. A *building* is made of many materials (e.g., wood, steel, plaster, etc.) and various structural elements. Each of those materials and elements are joined *together* to uphold the entirety of the structure they are a part of. In each example, the various parts, whether they are few or many, depend on each other to carry out the purpose of the whole.

Of course, God has a purpose for His people. Though much could be said about it, that purpose and mission can be summed up in two words as Jesus stated: *make disciples.*[181] That is, create other devoted followers of Jesus. A disciple is a lifelong learner and adherent (cooperative follower) to the teachings of another. In the case of Christ followers, that would be Jesus Christ and the Bible. In Luke 19:10, Jesus summed His entire reason for leaving the glory, comforts, and wonder of heaven and becoming one of us.[182] He said, "For the Son of Man came to seek and to save the lost."

Making disciples begins with sharing the gospel of forgiveness for those who repent (i.e., determine to turn from sin with God's help) and place personal faith in Jesus Christ alone for their salvation. Once someone decides to follow Jesus as He is revealed in the Bible, they have just begun what is a *lifelong* journey.

As a *physical* union between a man and a woman often leads to a *physical* birth, so a *spiritual* union of faith in Christ brings a *spiritual* birth. This is why Jesus called it being "born again."[183] As in the physical world, so in the spiritual world, the birth itself is just the beginning. Parents then have to spend huge amounts of time, energy, and finances to train that child through all their years into adulthood. It is no different spiritually. Spiritual parents (the one or ones who lead a person to repentance from sin and personal faith in Jesus Christ) have an even *greater* responsibility to see that the newborn Christ follower develops into a fully functioning, Spirit-filled and Spirit-led, follower of Jesus Christ. This takes the same elements of time, energy, and even finances to accomplish it well.

Can a person not attached to a local congregation do this? Yes and no. Think through this with me. While they can lead someone to faith in Christ and even help them learn to follow Him to a degree, part of that is reaching others. What will the independent follower do when that begins to happen? What about when those whom the convert reaches begin to reach others and so forth? What about when they bring their spouses, children, other relatives and associates to learn more? How will their spiritual needs be met without organization somewhere along the line? With so many varying opinions and views, how will it be determined exactly *what* they will be taught doctrinally?

Further, how will the independent believer fulfill Jesus' clear command to make disciples *of all nations* and preach the good news to every *person*[184] without aligning with an organization? Missionaries to those nations are appointed through a series of training and approval by their denomination or organization. Of course, that is necessary to insure that the person(s) being sent is committed, called by God, has the character, as well as the proper skills to live among another people group and be effective at ministering to them. In time, that would lead to all the issues above, wouldn't it? How would the independent believer help the gospel get to those people? This takes a huge amount of money and dedication to send them. Would a missionary move to another land without that support? Not one with a decent level of intelligence!

As we consider all of this, it becomes rather obvious that, while an independent Christian can touch others for Jesus, they cannot possibly be *as* effective at advancing the causes of Christ as the one who commits to a local, well-organized, Bible teaching congregation. The local church is designed to help people become followers of Jesus Christ, mature in that experience, and help others to do the same. After careful consideration, the local church, even with all her flaws and issues, is clearly the place that is done the *most* effectively.

DOES THE NEW TESTAMENT PROCLAIM A NEED FOR ORGANIZATION?

"I don't believe in organized religion." That's a popular thought. I think I understand what those who say this mean, but I am always a little amused by it.

I usually then ask them, "Do you mean you prefer *dis*organized religion?" Of course, we usually end up chuckling together.

Though there are other reasons, one thing seems to really spark this idea. We picture Jesus and His early followers as walking across the Middle East, ministering as they went, opposing the religious leaders of their time, and not being attached to one specific local synagogue. However, that's not the whole scenario. The Master opposed the *hypocritical* leaders of the Jewish faith, not the sincere ones who were honestly trying to live out their faith.[185] Also, the fact that Jesus and His followers were so often *in* the synagogue shows clearly that they were indeed committed to the flow of Jewish spiritual life.

It is also important to understand that the era of Jesus' personal ministry was a different season meant to launch the church age. The king had come to establish how His kingdom would operate on earth. This was to be the fulfillment of the Old Testament. He came to die for the sins of the world and be raised from the dead for the justification of those who would submit their very lives to Him. He also came to establish His church that would be the primary vehicle to proclaim His gospel in this world.

In his letter to the Christ followers in the ancient city of Ephesus, Paul the Apostle wrote, "Together [there's that word again!], we are His house, built on the foundation of the apostles and the prophets. And the cornerstone is Christ Jesus Himself."[186] A house is an organized structure with each part relying on the others to do their job. The apostles were the first leaders and elders of the church. They mentored other leaders to hand off the church to when their time in this world was completed. This would secure the establishment and mission Christ intended for His people to continue. Thus leaders are seen as a foundational part in the structure of the church.

In the book of Acts, Luke tells us about a problem the early church faced. In the distribution of food to their widows, one group was being neglected. The apostles called a meeting of all the Christ followers, and eventually, seven men were chosen to help oversee the task of the food distribution. This satisfied the church at large, met the needs of all the widows, and freed up the elders to keep their focus on "prayer and teaching the word."[187] These seven were the first deacons in the church. Besides the elders, they were the first people assigned to an office and given a title. The qualifications for elders, as well as deacons, are clearly stated in the New Testament.[188] It says that church leaders are *gifts* from Christ Himself to help govern His people in local congregations.[189] The spiritual leadership of the church was delegated to the elders, generation after generation, to lead the people of their time into the things of God. This ensured that the light of the gospel would never be snuffed out.

If God does not care about the church being organized, why does His Word so clearly call for a leadership structure, give qualifications, and even give them specific titles? Leaders were established in every local congregation of God's people. They are addressed or referred to over and over again throughout the New Testament. If God did not care if His people were part of His local established congregations, why would He record all that in His Word? Nowhere is it stated (or even implied) that said structure was just for *some* of His people and not others. If that were so, why doesn't His Word contain any examples, not even one, of Him being pleased with one of Christ's followers who was not part of the local church? Isn't the answer rather obvious? It was never His intention nor design.

HOW DO BELIEVERS MATURE THE MOST?

Birth may be the end of a pregnancy, but it is only the beginning of one's life. Birth is not the goal, just a preliminary step toward it. Every parent has hopes and dreams for their children. To see those things realized takes great effort, sacrifice, and diligence. Maturity is the process in which children develop into productive and contributing adult members of society. This is also true spiritually. God never intended that His people come to His Son to receive salvation and then just stay in that infantile stage. The goal is plain and singular. "That we will be mature in the Lord... growing in every way *more and more like Christ* [emphasis added], who is the head of His body, the church."[190]

As I have already mentioned in this book, I am the proud father of three sons. I have thoroughly enjoyed the maturity of my two older sons, Seth and Caleb. I fondly recall many vivid mental pictures of each of their stages of growth. Each stage had its joys and sorrows, but *far* more joy. It would take another book to record all the memories I have of their development.

Ezra, our youngest son with special needs, has been a different story. Though we love him intensely, his issues have created an enormous struggle for our family. His development has taken a different track than his two older siblings.

There are certain things that are normal for certain stages of life. We expect a baby to need their diaper changed. We expect a two-year-old to enjoy firmly saying no over and over. It's normal for thirteen-year-old to begin to be more interested in the opposite sex. (Many more examples could be given, but by now, you get the point.) However, to see these same behaviors at ages far removed from the norm is upsetting and a sign that something is wrong. This is how it is with Ezra, and it can also be that way spiritually.

Certain things are characteristic of a brand-new believer in Christ, a zeal for God's word usually accompanied by a lack of wisdom. This often causes the convert to be a bit obnoxious or even rude in the name of being bold. As they mature spiritually, the zeal shouldn't diminish and the wisdom should grow, often accompanied by apologies along the way.

Since maturity demonstrated in being *more and more like Christ* is the goal, we need to ask, what provides the elements most needed to make that goal the most likely to be realized? Some of the elements for maturity in this world are a healthy diet, a reasonable amount of rest, sufficient support, sound mentorship, quality education, physical exercise, and decent relationships. The parallel to spiritual maturity seems easily detectable here.

If we want that new believer (or even seasoned ones) to develop into a more Christlike person, those same elements are needed in the spiritual world. Let's consider them here but at the end of each category, *honestly* ask yourself this: Are these elements for spiritual maturity best supplied and developed in a local congregation with trained, anointed leaders, and a committed group of Christ followers with whom one is in an ongoing relationship or on one's own with interjections from others outside of an assembly committed to God and their community?

A healthy diet. For the Christ follower, this is a balanced intake of the Word of God. Much of this we feed ourselves. However, we need it taught to us from others with more experience and insight then we have. Obviously, the more experienced and educated the one who teaches, the more wisdom and understanding we will obtain. Of course, truth can best be applied in our lives with the help of someone who knows us and walks with us through life.

A reasonable amount of rest. Life is filled with turmoil. The greatest and deepest rest for the soul is only found in Jesus Christ. The teachings of Christ and all the Scriptures are the greatest resources known to humanity to obtain such rest. Hearing the stories of how others found that same peace at their moment of faith and throughout life can be a great source of spiritual strength and encouragement.

Sufficient support. "We all fall down," the old children's song says. How true! Thus the need to be lifted back up. There's nothing like having a place for shelter and being encouraged by people of similar passion for the Lord, sharing the common struggles of being human and a commitment to God and to one another.

Sound mentorship. This is being taught, encouraged, and coached by someone like us who has walked through the same issues and found reasonable answers to their struggles. Mentorship is really a more modern word for discipleship, which is the primary call to all Christ followers.[191]

Quality education. Would you attend (or send your children to) a school where the teachers were not educated? Of course not! Why? Because you would want the education to be from someone who knows what they're talking about. In the spiritual realm, this doesn't just mean those who have been schooled in a formal education, although that is certainly a good thing. Rather, it means those who have developed in their understanding of Scripture, the ways of God in life, and know how to apply all that effectively.

Activity/exercise. Faith is like a muscle. It needs pressure against it to grow strong. Spiritually speaking, we must put what we have learned to the test. When my kids learned to ride their bikes, I was trotting right on their side to make sure they were safe. When we put our training into practice, it's best to have someone trotting alongside us who has already made the journey, don't you think?

Let's be reasonable. Can you find all that without being dedicated to a local church? Of course you can. However, can you find all that at its *greatest* level without a local church? Absolutely not. Also, each of us is to contribute in all these areas to the development of others. Where is that best accomplished?

There is great spiritual safety in the context of a local group of caring Christ followers. One church sign I saw sure gives us pause to think about this. It read, "Remember the banana. When he left the bunch, he got skinned!" That's what the enemy of your soul would like to do to you and your spiritual growth!

Small-group teaching and interaction provide the opportunity to learn, grow, and find support in the context of God-honoring relationships. The "well-thought-out and practiced" music of a church praise team, leader, and/or choir provide a great opportunity for corporate worship. The weekly biblical messages proclaimed from the pulpit of a good Bible-teaching church through educated people of God whose gift was recognized, acknowledged, and affirmed by their elders are a healthy source of spiritual food. Times of prayer bring God's gentle help through His people, as well as a guide in how to develop one's own prayer life. The activities provided for people of various ages all bring more context and opportunity to express what we have been taught and to do so in a safe and supportive environment. The place of credible, established ministry, and effective witness provide the opportunity (using this word a lot here!) for you to bring others under all the same influence. Where is that best accomplished? Is that hard to answer?

For the Christ follower, even more important questions are, where does the Bible direct us to see those things occur? What did the early church do to see people mature spiritually?

The book of Acts is a historical record of the activities and priorities of the first century church. Consider this summary of the life of Jesus' first followers just after His return to heaven:

All the believers devoted themselves to the apostles'
teaching, and to *fellowship*, and to *sharing* in meals
[including the Lord's Supper], and to prayer. A deep sense
of awe came over them all, and the apostles performed
many miraculous signs and wonders. And *all the believers
met together* in *one* place and *shared everything* they had.
They sold their property and possessions and *shared* the
money with those in need. They worshiped *together* at the
Temple each day, met in homes for the Lord's Supper, and
shared their meals with great joy and generosity—all the
while praising God and enjoying the goodwill of all the
people. And each day the Lord added to their *fellowship*
those who were being saved.[192] [emphasis added]

Allow me to break that down. There's an entire book in this
passage, but let me just draw out a few notable things for our
discussion. It was *all* the believers. Also note that they were
devoted to certain things. This is a serious and diligent dedication.
They were devoted to *the apostles' teaching*. Where would they get
that? By gathering together with the apostles, of course. They
were also devoted to *fellowship*. This is spending time with other
believers. It also says that *all the believers met together in one place*.
They did not stay home, read their Bible, pray, and consider that
good enough. Nor did they meet in different places that they
chose on their own. No, it says that they worshipped *together at
the temple each day*. And as if that were not enough, they met in
each other's homes for the Lord's Supper, which was far more
than the present receiving of a cracker (or wafer) with some grape
juice in a thimble-sized cup that lasts about five minutes. It was a
fellowship *meal* shared by all. They *shared* their meals. That cannot
be done without being *together* often.

People were drawn to this community of believers. This is why
it says *the Lord added to their fellowship those who were being saved*.
These italicized words refer to their local assembly of believers
plainly. If not, then to what or whom do they refer?

If you are a professing Christ follower, is it not obvious these things are all best accomplished in the local church with God-ordained leaders watching over the souls of those for whom they will give an account?[193] Fellow follower, can I be candid? It takes some serious theological fancy-footwork mixed with human carnality to say that these things are all best realized outside the local church. Or worse yet, to suggest that this was not (or is not now) God's obvious plan. If you would even hesitate to agree with what the Bible clearly teaches here, I would suggest you have been deceived.

Now before you throw the book down and stop reading, please very carefully read the next two questions and the corresponding discussions that follow.

STRANGE FIRE: WHAT'S THAT?

Strobe candles were pretty popular in the late sixties when I was a kid. The flicker of the light was thought to relax people. I will always remember the first time I saw someone using one.

I shared a bedroom with my older brother Charlie, who is nine years my senior. I was about ten years old when I walked into our room to find him sitting on the edge of his bed in the lotus position with a psychedelic light wheel spinning and the strobe candle lit. In his search for truth, he got into the Self-Realization Fellowship[194] as well as Transcendental Meditation.[195]

I tried to talk to him, and he seemed unable to communicate. He was in some kind of a trance. I called his name several times while standing right in front of him, but he was completely unresponsive. It spooked me so badly that I ran out of the room. The lights, the fire, my brother's condition, and everything surrounding that situation were the strangest things I had encountered in my young life. Let me tell you about another strange fire.

To help Moses oversee the people of ancient Israel, God gave him his brother Aaron as well as his sons to help him. In chapters eight and nine of Leviticus,[196] God instructed Moses how to ordain the priests to minister properly in the Tabernacle. Long story short, at the end of chapter nine, once all the proper procedures, clothing, and offerings were sufficiently ready, the glory of God expressed in fire consumed the sacrifices. Suddenly, fire blazed forth from the Lord in a notable display of His glory! The people's reaction was amazed adoration. The Scriptures proclaim, "When the people saw this, they shouted with joy and fell face down on the ground [in worship]."[197] Aaron's two oldest sons, Nadab and Abihu, thought the experience was so incredible that they tried to reproduce it *their own way*. This is where the story takes a turn for the worst.

In the very next chapter, the Bible reveals their actions. Leviticus 10:1 says, "Then Nadab and Abihu, the sons of Aaron, each took his censer and put fire in it, put incense on it, and offered profane fire before the Lord, which He had not commanded them."

The word *profane* is an interesting one. The King James Version translates it as *strange* while the English Standard Version states it as *unauthorized*. It means "strange; stranger [or] to become estranged."[198] Basically, their self-styled maverick worship was estranged from the way God had directed them to honor Him. They deliberately violated His revealed procedures for approaching Him, so He determined that their worship was *profane*. It was strange because the very God they were trying to worship had not authorized their method.

Of course, their approach to Him led to them being estranged from God Himself. Watch God's response in the next verse: "So fire went out from the Lord and devoured them, and they died before the Lord." Wow!

In the letter to the Romans, the apostle Paul tells us that "the wages *[payment; end result]* of sin is death."[199] Sin is to violate the known will of God. Certainly, to know how God has taught people to worship and to come up with one's own way is to violate the will of God stated plainly in His word. This is sin, and it offends our Creator.

Further, James told us in the first chapter of his letter, "Then, when desire has conceived, it gives birth to sin; and sin, when it is full-grown, brings forth death."

Both passages tell us plainly that sin always leads to death, if it isn't turned away from. Since people don't typically die *physically* at the moment they sin, it must refer to some other *kind* of death—that death is a spiritual one, separation from God. In human relationships, sinning against another (willfully violating their known will) will bring separation between the two parties. It's the same with God. This is what happened to Nadab and Abihu. They became a powerful example of what will happen to those who disregard what the very God they're supposedly trying to worship has directed. Fire will eventually devour them and the spiritual separation (death) they taste on earth will then play out in everlasting spiritual death. In other words, they will be separated from the One they sinned against. In application, we would be wise to be sure our worship of God is done the way He has instructed!

How would you answer the question, "Is your worship of God in agreement with His instructions, or do you worship God *your* way?" If it isn't God's way, you're offering strange, unauthorized, and profane worship to Him. Since it led to the estrangement of these men from God, why would it be any different for you? After seeing what happened to Aaron's two sons, do you really want to continue in that trajectory? I strongly urge you to come to the God of the Bible through His Son Jesus Christ and get in sync with a congregation of those who do the same!

ARE YOU RAISING CAIN?

The very first expressions of worship in the Bible are found in Genesis. The first couple, Adam and Eve, had many children, but the first mention of worship involves their two oldest sons—Cain and Abel. Their parents had taught them what God had demonstrated to atone for *their* original sin. After their defiance of God's single command came to light and he confronted them, as well as the serpent, Genesis 3:21 states, "And the Lord God made clothing from animal skins for Adam and his wife." This was the first shedding of blood for sin.

While humanity may take sin somewhat lightly, the Holy God of scripture, evidently, does not. This principle of the shedding of blood to atone for sin began right there and followed clear through history to the sacrifice of Christ Himself for the sins of humanity. Hebrews 9:22 states, "Without the shedding of blood, there is no forgiveness of sin."[200] Into that setting stepped Cain and Abel.

As the first two brothers grew up, Abel (the younger) became a keeper of livestock, while Cain was more of an agricultural tiller of the ground—i.e., a farmer. Let's look at Genesis 4 to see the story.

> When it was time for the harvest, Cain presented *some* of his crops as a gift to the Lord. Abel also brought a gift—the *best* of the *firstborn* lambs from his flock. The Lord accepted Abel and his gift, but he did not accept Cain and his gift. This made Cain very angry, and he looked dejected. (emphasis added)

On the surface, this looks like nothing more than favoritism, and frankly, God seems unfair. However, what has happened here is that, though their parents educated them that God required blood sacrifices, Cain decided he would worship God his own way. He was a farmer and so bringing what came from his labor and abilities seemed better to him than what God had instituted. He felt what he gave God should have been good enough, so he was very angry.

Knowing what his anger would lead to, God tried to correct and instruct him,

> "Why are you so angry?" the Lord asked Cain. "Why do you look so dejected? You will be accepted if you do what is right." [clearly showing that what he did was not "right," comment added] But if you refuse to do what is right, then watch out! Sin is crouching at the door, eager to control you. But you must subdue it and be its master.

God gave human beings a free will. Cain had a choice to make. He could admit he had done wrong and then bring the right offering. Or continue in his stubborn rebellion and let sin subdue and master him. Unfortunately, he chose the latter.

The expression of his anger was jealousy and rage that led to deception, guile, and the first murder. The next verse in Genesis 4 says, "One day Cain suggested to his brother, 'Let's go out into the fields.' And while they were in the field, Cain attacked his brother, Abel, and killed him."

The Apostle John commented on this event centuries later. Under the inspiration of the Holy Spirit he wrote,

> We must not be like Cain, who belonged to the evil one and killed his brother. And why did he kill him? Because Cain *had been doing* what was evil, and his brother had been doing what was righteous.[201] (emphasis added)

Please note that these refer to an ongoing pattern; i.e., a lifestyle.

This dastardly deed was born from a heart that felt he could worship God his own way. There's a spiritual application here. I have noticed how professing followers of Christ who want little or nothing to do with the local church also get very angry when confronted with the truth of God's Word. If they could, it seems that some would get rid of the local church or organized religion so they could worship God their own way.

The writer of the letter to the Hebrews further adds:

> It was by *faith* that Abel brought *a more acceptable offering* to God than Cain did. Abel's offering gave evidence that he was a righteous man, and God showed His approval of his gifts. Although Abel is long dead, he still speaks to us by his example of faith.[202] (emphasis added)

How does Abel still speak to us? His example instructs us not to follow the pattern of his murderous brother, no matter the cost. God has told us how He wants to be worshipped, and no matter how good our intentions or how popular another approach may be, it will not be acceptable to God.

Jack Hayford put it plainly and well in his great book *The Reward of Worship*. He states,

> In my own nation, the culture of our politics has strangely played into the idea that "I can decide how to worship God on my own." There is nothing in the Bible that says we can approach God in worship on our own terms—ever.[203]

Friend, Cain has been dead for millennia. However, if someone is using his approach to worship the God of the Bible, they are *raising Cain* back to life. The result will be the same—God's disapproval. Like Cain, one stuck in this pattern will be accepted if they do what is right. That is, come to God on *His* terms, not their own.

The Bible shows that the only sacrifice for our sins that is acceptable to Him is the blood of His sinless Son. Sin is defined as any thought, word, deed or lack of required action that is less than God's perfect will. The Scriptures show that one sin disqualifies us from God's perfect heaven.[204] The standard to get close to God and enter heaven? According to Jesus, it is to "be perfect."[205] I know, impossible, right? By your own good deeds, religious actions, or your own character, correct! God knew this, and that is why, out of amazing love and grace toward us, He became one of us in the person of Jesus, came, and lived a life like ours and died as our substitute. He bore the penalty for all the sins of every human being so that those who come to Him and surrender to His Lordship will not have to pay for it all themselves in hell for all of eternity.

We can either be like Abel, who relied on the blood sacrifice that he had been taught God would accept. Or we can be like Cain and come up with our own way to worship God. These two brothers serve as examples of the only two approaches there can be to God and the only two results that occur—the approval and acceptance of God or the lack thereof.

Are you raising Cain, coming to God on your own terms? Or coming the way *He* said to? If you have attempted to come through Christ, how and where will you live out your faith? Will you attempt to do that within the local church as the Bible clearly teaches Christ's followers should or on your own? Like these two brothers, you have a choice to make.

7

THE CHALLENGE

THE BOTTOM LINE

This brief chapter turns a corner. I have written about clarifying which God you are honestly seeking. We then considered some of the obvious problems in the church. There are plenty. Anyone with eyes and any level of discernment knows this. I then presented some of the things I have seen happen on the positive end of those very same problems. In the previous three chapters, we considered a variety of issues and questions needing to be addressed to know if the God of the Bible has (or has not) ordained how He wants us to approach Him and how the local church may (or may not) fit in there.

CHURCH! WHO NEEDS IT?!

It has become very obvious that the local church is God's design. She is God's bride and *the* avenue through which He works on this earth. Even with all her flaws, she is "the church of the living God, which is the pillar and foundation of the truth."[206] In fact, in Paul's letter to the believers in the city of Ephesus, he said, "God's purpose in all this was to use *the church* [emphasis added] to display His wisdom in its rich variety to all."[207] This is just another reference to the church body as a whole. His collective bride is whom or what He reaches to this hurting world through. This is the only honest conclusion any person genuinely looking for the truth could come to in light of the scriptures.

Without any biblical record of God blessing a professing Christ follower who is independent, we can only conclude one of two things:

1. Either none existed and all who professed to follow Jesus understood the connection between faith in Him and commitment to His people; or
2. God did not or does not recognize such a person *as genuinely His.*

I am fully aware that a person becomes a child of God by grace through faith and not of their own works, deeds, or character.[208] However, I also know that the devil is a *master* deceiver who has been deceiving humans for thousands, consider that, *thousands of years*! Further, there is a level of faith that even he and his cohorts have *a faith that does not save the soul*[209] but salves the conscience just enough to cause one to think they are in right standing with God when the reality is they are not. That is a frightening place to be!

These recent previous paragraphs, even this entire book, is not about me winning an argument and convincing you to go to church (although I do hope you end up there). My hope is to see the multitude of people who profess a belief in the God of the Bible to examine if they are truly in the body of Christ as the

Lord defines in His word. Here's the culmination of the matter: I want to meet you in heaven someday.

Eternity is at stake here, not the purchase of a book or me making royalties on an interesting subject. The primary issue for me, the very purpose why I am convinced that the Lord put it in my heart to write this book is to see people who are deceived into thinking they know God be set free to *truly* know Him. To come into a right relationship with Him and be settled, stable, peaceful, and full of joy on their journey to His heavenly kingdom where I will meet them one day! This is all about you, yes, *you*!

Whether you agree or disagree, are you absolutely certain that what you believe agrees with God's revelation of truth? Are you so convinced that you are ready to stake your soul on it because ultimately that is what is being done? So many people throw around the word *believe*, giving it the shallow definition of simply giving mental assent to some facts. *That isn't biblical soul-saving faith.* That definition puts belief that George Washington walked this earth on the same level as believing in Christ. The only faith that *that* requires is to trust that historians recorded things accurately.

But the word *believe*, as it pertains to biblical truth and the receiving of salvation, refers to the person who "trusts in, clings to [and] relies on"[210] Jesus Christ as their Lord (i.e., master) and savior. As one man of God once wrote, "To believe in God's word means nothing more or less than to believe precisely as God has said."[211]

Another former college president wrote, "As we seek to know God, there must be no vacillation. *Our God must be the God of the Bible!*"[212] [emphasis added]

In his thought-provoking book, *What Jesus Demands From the World*, John Piper gives some good insight into what the Lord meant when telling a woman how to worship the God of the Bible. He said the "true worshipers will worship the Father in spirit and truth." He said to worship God in truth as Jesus said is to "bring your experience of worship into conformity with what is true about God...what matters now is not where you worship but whether you worship God in accordance with the truth."[213] Do you?

I knew when I started writing this book that there would be those who so disagree that they would put this book down in anger and refuse to read it further. However, if you have read this far, you have come face-to-face with the truth. If you are going to honestly follow the God of the Bible and His Son Jesus Christ, you need to be part of a local church. So what are you going to do about it? You are at a fork in the road, so to speak. You can either chose the more popular route, that is a profession in God that rejects His word, His clear plan and commitment to a local congregation. Or you can choose to obey His word, find a good Bible-teaching church, and jump in with both feet! I pray you chose the latter. You may be concerned about what people may think.

In his small booklet, *How to Fortify Your Faith*, Dr. Adrian Rogers says, "If you please God, it doesn't matter whom you displease. And if you displease God, it doesn't matter whom you please."[214] Further he states, "Selective obedience is not obedience at all."[215]

Perhaps when you started this book, you were (or are) one of the multitudes of people who profess to know Jesus but are detached from His church. If after reading this book and the scriptures that have been shared, you can continue in that vein, at best you are a disobedient Christian. At worst, you are not truly saved at all. In other words, the enemy of our souls has used every means at his disposal to trick you into continuing on a popular path that, when all is said and done, will damn your soul so that you join *him* in eternity. Horrific beyond description!

Wow, right to the point, huh? Actually, no. We've taken this entire book to get here! May I ask you a question as we come to the close of this journey together? Also, may I ask you to really think long and hard about your answer as well? Before I do, let me share with you a statistic that *every* human being (both living and dead) would agree on. No kidding, every rational human being agrees. It does not matter their socio-economic state, business savvy, educational level, marital status, religious views, philosophy, or any other category you could conceive or suggest. From the bush in the deepest part of Africa to the grandest mansion of the Caribbean, every single human being would agree with what I am about to state. Are you ready? Here it is: ten out of ten people die. True? Unless the coming of Jesus happens in our lifetime (and it very well may!), no one gets out of here alive—*no one.*

What's even more difficult is, with rare exception, no one has any idea or way of knowing when their last breath will be. That is not a scare tactic; it is a cold, hard reality that no reasonable person could prove flawed or wrong.

In light of these inarguable facts, doesn't it only make sense to do all you can to be as *certain* as you can that you and your loved ones are ready for this last journey? Remember, this is a journey from which no one returns. Okay, here are my questions:

1. If today were your day to leave this world and stand before God and He were to ask you, "Why should I let you in to My heaven?" what would you say? (Remember, it is *His* heaven, and He is not subject to popular ideas, majority opinion, or feelings, and He does not grade on the curve!) *Please* take some time to think through and answer that question before going to the next one.

2. Assuming you took the suggested time so that your answer to *this* question does not alter your *most honest* answer to the first, how many pronouns (I, me, etc.) were contained in your answer? Whoever you mentioned the most is who your trust is in to get you to heaven. Please be 100 percent honest. Was it *you* and *your* own goodness (i.e., "*I'm* a good person," "*I* don't hurt anyone," "*I'm* not a murderer," etc.)

or was it God and the substitutionary death, burial, and resurrection of His Son Jesus Christ?

If it were the latter, the gist of your answer to God's question would simply be, "Because I have trusted solely in the blood that Your Son shed for me at the cross, His resurrection, and Your grace as my only hope of salvation." According to the God of the Bible, a person can either trust themselves or Christ to obtain a relationship with God and entrance into His heaven *but not both*. Trusting in oneself is the only accurate definition of *self-righteousness*. The one who trusts only in the death, burial, and resurrection of Jesus Christ as their substitute is the only one *truly* righteous in the eyes of the Father. The reason is that they have accepted what can be called "the great exchange." They embrace the fact that Jesus took their sin, and they have received—please don't miss this—*His* righteousness. Righteousness, so far as God is concerned, is to be in right relationship with Him. This is accomplished through repentance from sin (a change of mind, heart and attitude toward it demonstrated by turning away from it) and faith in Jesus Christ as one's Lord (master) and, thus, Savior.

If you have realized that you have not done that, but would like to, please consider praying the following prayer from your heart. Please understand, there is no magic in these exact words. However, if they reflect what is in truly in your heart of hearts, you will begin a new relationship with God through His Son. You will receive eternal life at that moment of surrender to Him and the barrier of sin, which has blocked His best for you, will have been removed! Pray something like this out loud.

> Dear Father, I confess that I am a sinner and I need forgiveness. I believe that Jesus Christ is the Son of God and that He died for my sins. I believe that You raised Him from the dead on the third day and that He is my only but certain hope of receiving salvation. Jesus, please come into my life and forgive me for all my sins. With the

STEVE CRINO

help of Your Spirit and Your people, I will live for You from this day forward. Thank you for hearing and answering my simple but sincere prayer. Amen.

If you prayed that prayer with all your heart for the first time, please contact me through the information on the back cover of this book. I want to help you get plugged into a good church in your area. You are now part of a family, and you need to get connected with your brothers and sisters!

If you are already a Christ follower and plugged into your local church, I hope this book inspires you to realize the fathomless depth of the conflict for the souls of humanity that we are engaged in. I pray that you will realize that though we can certainly (and should!) have lots of fun along the way, *we best take this war seriously.* Be assured the enemy of our souls sure does! Will you? Do you know anyone who may benefit from this book? If so, would you please either give them this copy or buy them one?

So when everything is said and done, to answer the opening question and the title of this book, *Church! Who Needs It?!,* if you are a follower of Jesus Christ, *you* do! And the church needs *you!*

I'd like to close with the following that was contained in an e-mail from a friend. It is a great illustration to finish this book with.

A Churchgoer once wrote a letter to the editor of a newspaper and complained that it made no sense to go to church every Sunday. "I've gone for 30 years now," he wrote, "and in that time I have heard something like 3,000 sermons. But for the life of me, I can't remember a single one of them. So, I think I'm wasting my time and the pastors are wasting theirs by giving sermons at all."

This started a real controversy in the "Letters to the Editor" column, much to the delight of the editor. It went on for weeks until someone wrote this clincher: "I've been married for 30 years now. In that time my wife has cooked some 32,000 meals. But, for the life of me, I cannot recall the entire menu for a single one of those meals. But I do know this...they all nourished me and gave me the strength I needed to do my work. If my wife had not given me these meals, I would be physically dead today.

Likewise, if I had not gone to church for nourishment, I would be spiritually dead today! Thank God for our physical and spiritual nourishment!

AFTERWORD

ENCOURAGEMENT TO WOULD-BE WRITERS

It's trapped inside you, isn't it? If neither time nor money were an issue, and you could know your book would be appreciated, what subject would you write about? If there is something that immediately comes to your mind, you should probably write a book about it. There are experiences you have had and subjects you have gained some insight into that, if you wrote about them, could truly help people. So what are you waiting for? A sign from God? Well, I got mine to finish this book from a rather unorthodox source for a Bible-believing Christ follower. Nonetheless, I knew it was God. Let me tell you about it, and I hope it will encourage you to write the book you have always wanted to.

I was sitting around a large table with a bunch of other pastors and leaders from my denomination. We meet periodically in a sort of round-table discussion about issues that impact our leadership. Typically, our leader asks someone to come in and share some insight on something he feels we can all benefit from.

This particular month, it was another pastor, author, speaker, and friend Rev. Marios Ellinas. The topic of discussion was his third book, *The Next Test*.

Some of us there were would-be authors, and besides fielding our questions about tests in our lives and ministries, we also grilled him on the process of writing books. Marios encouraged us and told us basically, "There is something inside you that the rest of us need to know...things that will help us. You need to write that book."

Let me tell you, the book that you are holding took me far too long to write. I wrote it over about a ten-year span between three pastoral positions, attending seminary, raising a family, and planting a church from scratch. Though the subject and the gist of it has been in my spirit for years, I tried to write as one would treat a hobby—an hour here, two hours there, a day or so when I could squeeze it in, etc. It has been an immense pleasure and a major source of frustration at the same time because of one thing I seemed to really lack in order to complete the assignment—time.

So after the aforementioned leadership discussion, we all headed for a local Chinese restaurant for lunch and more discussion. I happened to sit across from Pastor Marios. As we talked over lunch, I shared my frustration at trying to finish this book, and I said something to the effect of, "I wonder if I'll ever get this done."

He again encouraged me and said, "You've got to do it, bro. We need what God has put in your heart." I agreed yet wondered if God really wanted me to do this, or was all this work over these years a complete waste of time. Would this book stay in a Word document on my computer and my descendants find it after I die or something? If only I could get some clear encouragement from God...then it happened.

Let me just tell you, I am not superstitious, and I am repulsed when people try to read something spiritual into every detail of life and every seeming coincidence. I do not carry a rabbit's foot, knock on wood, throw salt over my shoulder, or believe in palm reading or anything of the kind. However, what happened next, though it was simple and not dramatic in any way, it spoke right to my need, and I have no doubt it was God. It has never happened to me before, I am not sure it ever will again, and I do not recommend looking for "signs" or direction from God in this way; however, this is how God confirmed His will for me in this.

I finished my lunch and nonchalantly picked up my fortune cookie as we chatted. Just for the fun of it, I read the little paper from the cookie and was pleasantly astounded to read a sentence that gave me the sign of affirmation I needed. It simply said:

You are a lover of words…someday you will write a book.

Coincidence? I sure don't think so. What about you? Perhaps God is speaking to you to write something to help us all out too. Let me say it again: it's inside you, isn't it? So let me ask again, if neither time nor money were an issue and you could know your book would be appreciated, what subject would you write about? If there is something that immediately comes to mind, you should probably write a book about it. Come on, friend, go for it! Why not get started today?

Home Depot says, "You can do it, and we can help." Is the Lord saying to you, "You can do it, and I can help"? I hope so. I want to hear what He has deposited in you to invest in humanity. To quote Nike, "Just do it!"

NOTES

Preface

1. I give credit for this idea to Paul Rieser from his book *Couplehood*. He did this in the opening of his book, and I thought it was both clever and funny!

2. Neil Anderson, Victory Over the Darkness, Second Edition (Ventura, California: Regal Books [a division of Gospel Light], 2000), 101.

The Core

3. George Barna, "How Post-Christian is America?", Barna Group, [Note insert access or modification date in month/day/year format], https://www.barna.org/barna-update/culture/608-hpca#.UlLT_FOkSwc.

4. Lead singer of the band Harvest.

The Clarity

5. See John 3:2.

6. Means "from above" and refers to a resurrection of one's spirit, which is dead in sin (Eph. 2:1) before this experience only God can bring about (John 1:12–13).

7. See Genesis 3.

8. See Romans 5:12 and note the word *because*. Also, Romans 5:18–19 noting the shift from the word *all* to *many*, implying a volitional choice to identify with both the first and second Adam.

9. See the Romans 3:23 and the letter from James 1:15.

10. See the letter to the Ephesians 2:1 and following.

11. See the book of the Revelation 21:27.

12. The Greek is plural, meaning Jesus saying this applies to everyone.

13. Greek is *mōria* from the root word *mōros* alluding to being *moronic* and plainly meaning *foolishness*.

14. By "physical birth," I am referring to *biological* birth. Adoption certainly qualifies for one to be called *father*.

15. Edward W. Goodrick and John R. Kohlenberger, *The NIV Exhaustive Concordance* (Grand Rapids, Michigan: Zondervan, 1990), 200.

16. David Noel Freedman, Astrid B. Beck, Allen C. Myers, eds., *Eerdmans Dictionary of the Bible* (Grand Rapids, Michigan: Eerdmans Publishing, 2000), 252.

17. See Acts 20:21.

18. See 1 John 3:5–9.

19. See Ephesians 2:1 and following.

20. I.e., agreement, contract, or testament.

21. See John 1:12–13 and the letter from 1 Peter 1:3.

22. See Ephesians 5:23.

23. Acts is a Spirit-inspired historical record of the first-century church.

24. See 1 Corinthians 6:17.

25. See Hebrews 11:10.

The Quandary

26. John Wesley quoted in the book "Discovering Ezekiel and Daniel," page 65. Published by uideposts Associates, Inc., Carmel, NY; General Editor, Floyd W. Thatcher
27. See Ephesians 5:25.
28. http://en.wikipedia.org/wiki/What's_Love_Got_to_Do_with_It_(song) September 25, 2007
29. See 1 John 4:8.
30. See John 13:8.
31. See Acts 11:26 and understand this was a derogatory term mocking Jesus' followers as "little Christs."
32. See James 1:8.
33. Spence, H. D. M., *The Pulpit Commentary, Volume 17: Gospel of John*, vol. 2, 1977: 196, quoted in Tertullian and Menucius Felix, *Tertullian Apologetical Work and Minucius Felix Octavius [The Fathers of the Church, A New Translation]*, vol. 10, translated by Rudolph Arbesmann, Sister Emily Joseph Daly, Edwin A. Quain (Washington, D.C.: Catholic University of America Press [in association with Consortium Books], 1977).
34. Pharisees were a group of hypocritical Jewish leaders with an overly strict system of behavior. They looked down on anyone and everyone who didn't adhere to all they taught.
35. http://en.wikipedia.org/wiki/Where's_the_beef%3F October 9, 2007
36. Pam Stenzel, Sex, Love & Relationships, Session 3—The Spiritual Experiences, Vision Video Inc.
37. See Genesis 1:26–27.
38. See Genesis 1–2.
39. See Exodus 15.
40. See Joshua 6.

41. John Garstang and J. B. E. Garstang, *The Story of Jericho*, rev. ed. (London and Edinburgh: Marshall, Morgan & Scott, LTD., 1948), 136.

42. Flavius Josephus, "The Antiquities of the Jews," in *The Works of Josephus: Complete and Unabridged in One Volume, New Updated Edition*. 13th printing. Translated by William Whiston (Peabody, MA: Hendrickson Publishers, 1998), book 5, chap. 1, sec. 6.

43. See 1 Corinthians 15:3–7.

44. "Relevance." *The American Heritage® Dictionary of the English Language, Fourth Edition*. Houghton Mifflin Company, 2004. 25 Oct. 2007. <Dictionary.com http:// dictionary.reference.com/browse/Relevance>.

45. http://www.mcdonalds.com/corp/about.html–retrieved on Friday, October 26, 2007.

46. As long as it is modest, see 1 Timothy 2:9a.

47. *Gospel* means "good news"!

48. Dictionary.com, s.v. "hypocrite," accessed February 5, 2008, <Dictionary.com http://dictionary.reference.com/browse/ Hypocrite>.

49. Ibid.

50. See Philippians 2:5–8 in the New Testament.

51. He is often called St. John or John the Beloved.

52. See John 8:12.

53. See 1 Thessalonians 5:2.

54. See Matthew 24:43.

55. See 1 Peter 1:15–16 as well the letter from James 3:1.

56. See 1 John 1:7.

57. "About James Randi," James Randi Educational Foundation, accessed January 31, 2010, http://www.randi.org/site/index. php/about-james-randi.html.

58. http://www.veoh.com/browse/videos/category/peo-ple_and_blogs/watch/v17922446wYsEsNtY= Viewed on January 28, 2010 at 10:20 p.m. EST.

59. See the Acts 20:29–31a.
60. See Matthew chapter 7, verses 15–23.
61. *Sybil, IMDb,* accessed January 13, 2009, http://www.imdb.com/title/tt0075296/.
62. "Lutheran Church Denomination: Overview of the Lutheran Church," *Christianity.about.com,* accessed February 15, 2009, http://christianity.about.com/od/lutherandenomination/p/lutheranprofile.htm.
63. http://www.wels.net/cgi-bin/site.pl–Sunday, February 15, 2009
64. See Luke 23:34.
65. See John 17:21–23.
66. See Ephesians 4:5.
67. John 8:32.
68. See Jeremiah 29:13.
69. See Jeremiah 33:3.

The Counteraction

70. See Proverbs 18:17.
71. "Wapakoneta, Ohio," *City-data.com,* accessed February 17, 2009, http://www.city-data.com/city/Wapakoneta-Ohio.html.
72. "Introduction," *NASA Apollo 11 30th Anniversary,* accessed February 27, 2009, http://history.nasa.gov/ap11ann/introduction.htm.
73. *The Physics Factbook,* s.v. "space shuttle," accessed February 15, 2009, http://hypertextbook.com/facts/1998/ColinLew.shtml.
74. Accessed February 27, 2009, http://www.google.com/search?hl=en&q=horsepower&aq=0&oq=Horsep.
75. *The Physics Factbook,* s.v. "space shuttle," accessed February 15, 2009, http:// hypertextbook.com/facts/1998/ColinLew.shtml.

76. What follows is the original submission of my story now contained in Bob Strand's book *In the Company of Angels*.

77. This is the end of the original submission of my story now edited and contained in Bob Strand's book *In the Company of Angels*.

78. See 1 Corinthians 6:19–20.

79. The verse in 2 Corinthians 5:17 says, "Anyone who belongs to Christ has become a new person. The old life is gone; a new life has begun" (New Living Translation)!

80. Neil Anderson, *Victory Over the Darkness*, Second Edition (Ventura, California: Regal Books [a division of Gospel Light], 2000),119.

81. By the term *Christian*, I refer to those who have surrendered their lives to the Lord Jesus Christ as he is revealed in the Bible, have repented of their sin, trusted him as savior and Lord, and have been genuinely born again (John 3:3–7). It is critical to note here that not all that attend a church or religious services are Christians as the Bible defines one.

82. Acts 11:26.

83. "Tacitus on Christ," *Wikipedia*, accessed April 4, 2013, http://en.wikipedia.org/wiki/Tacitus_on_Christ.

84. John 13:35.

85. 1 John 4:19–21.

86. 1 John 4:8.

87. "I Still Haven't Found What I'm Looking For" from U2's *The Joshua Tree* album.

88. See Revelation 22:17.

89. "Relevance." *The American Heritage® Dictionary of the English Language, Fourth Edition*. Houghton Mifflin Company, 2004. 25 Oct. 2007. <Dictionary.com http://dictionary.reference.com/browse/Relevance>.

90. Genesis means "book of beginnings."

91. See Genesis 12:14.

92. See Genesis 12:20.

93. See Genesis 25:21–26.
94. See Genesis 25:27.
95. See Genesis 27:5–40.
96. See Genesis 27:41–45.
97. See Acts 7:22. Moses wrote the first five books in the Bible (referred to as the Pentateuch).
98. See 1 Kings 3:12.
99. See Colossians 4:14. Luke (who was a physician) wrote the Gospel of Luke, as well as the book of Acts.
100. See Acts 22:3. Paul was trained by Gamaliel, the most highly respected rabbi of the first century.
101. With over fifty years of experience, I encourage anyone struggling with an addiction to contact Teen Challenge at http://teenchallengeusa.com/
102. These facts emerge in the book *The Jesus Factor* by David Manuel published by Logos International in 1977.
103. "Prophetic" refers to utterances inspired by God that are either forthtelling or foretelling concerning things the speaker does not know in his or her natural abilities or intellect.
104. Those who rarely commit to any local church because they are always going where they "feel" God or have some kind of thrilling experience. Though they sound spiritual, they actually weaken the local church.
105. See Matthew 28:19–20 in the New Testament.
106. See Hebrews 10:24.
107. See James 5:16.
108. Our church and our family are forever indebted to these individuals who were the foundation of our church!
109. People often do acts of service because it makes them feel good. If that's the primary motive, then the supposed act of service is actually selfish, though it does not appear so.
110. To read about Joni's story, go to http://www.joniareckson-tadastory.com/

111. For more information on Joni's ministry, go to http://www.joniandfriends.org/
112. When a new church is *birthed* out of another, that church is known as the *mother church* and the new one a *daughter church.*
113. *Dictionary.com,* s.v. "denomination," August 20, 2010, http://dictionary.reference.com/browse/denomination.
114. One exception would be the Lutheran church, taking their name from Martin Luther.
115. *Dictonary.com,* s.v. "doctrine," accessed September 23, 2010, http://dictionary.reference.com/browse/Doctrine?&qsrc=
116. L. Morris, "Church Government", *BELIEVE Religious Information Source - By Alphabet,* accessed November 28, 2010, http://mb-soft.com/believe/text/cgovern.htm.

The Questions

117. For 120 years, while the ark was being built, God's gracious offer of safety in the ark was given to any who would repent of sin and trust in Him. (See Genesis 6:3 and the surrounding account.)
118. See Romans 3:23–26.
119. The equivalent in the New Testament era would be a church.
120. See Peter 2:21.
121. *Apostles* means "sent ones."
122. Luke is the third gospel and book of the New Testament.
123. This quote is from Acts 1:4–5.
124. See Jude 12 English Standard, King James, and New King James Versions of the Bible
125. This is how it's worded in the New Living Translation.
126. See 2 Thessalonians 1:4, Galatians 1:2 and 22, just to name a few.
127. I usually use the words *Christ follower* and avoid the word *Christian* because the latter has come to mean little in the Western world. "Christian" means "little Christ" and was

actually a derogatory term coined to ridicule the followers of Jesus Christ for being so like him. In the mind of many in the West in our modern world, however, it refers to a moral person who intellectually assents to a belief in God.

128. See 1 Kings 17 and James 5:17.

129. See 1 Kings 17:8–16.

130. See 1 Kings 17: 17–24.

131. See 2 Kings 1:9–15.

132. Jesus' half-brother; see Galatians 1:19.

133. See Hebrews 10:25 in the New Living Translation (NLT),

134. NIV

135. Accessed December 1, 2011, http://thinkexist.com/ quotation/the_bible_knows_nothing_of_solitary_ religion/295382.html.

136. The more detailed story is on page 55.

137. *Bible Study Tools,* s.v. [Note: "koinonia,"] accessed April 5, 2013, http://www.biblestudytools.com/lexicons/greek/kjv/ koinonia.html.

138. See Acts 2:42.

139. See http://finance.yahoo.com/news/pf_article_102425. html viewed on Thursday, February 6, 2014.

140. Genesis 1:26.

141. See Genesis 1:27; 1 Corinthians 11:7; James 3 verse, etc.

142. Genesis 1:1.

143. John 1:1.

144. See John 5:18, 8:51–58, and 10:30.

145. Genesis 1:2.

146. See Acts 5:1–11 for one of them.

147. Deuteronomy 4:35, 39; 32:39; 1 Kings 8:60; Isaiah 43:10– 11, 44:6–8, 45:5, 6 and 14, and many passages.

148. 1 John 4:8.

149. 1 Peter 1:15–17.

150. Ephesians 5:1–2.

151. 1 John 1:7.

STEVE CRINO

152. Unless, of course, one is physically unable or deterred by some inescapable circumstances that truly could not be overcome.
153. See Genesis 14:20.
154. See Genesis 28:22.
155. See Matthew 23:23 and Luke 11:42.
156. Matthew 6:2.
157. Temple and synagogue in the Old Testament and the church in the New Testament.
158. Genesis 14:19–21.
159. Genesis 28:20–22.
160. See the book of Malachi 3:6–11.
161. See Matthew 23:23 and Luke 11:42.
162. Note that the majority of times the scriptures direct believers to support the poor it is to help those of the covenant community first. There is no evidence that God's intent was that the church become a public welfare system.
163. Also see Romans 12:3–8 and 1 Corinthians 12.
164. See Matthew 28:18–20.
165. See Matthew 10:1–5.
166. See 1 Corinthians 15:6–8.
167. See 1 Corinthians 12:27–14:33 where Paul is establishing order in congregational gatherings.
168. See Ephesians 2:20. Jesus' apostles and the Old Testament prophets set the foundation for the church. Their words carried the same authority as scripture does now.
169. See Acts 6:5–6, 8:4–8, 21:8.
170. Dictionary.com, s.v. "pastor," accessed June 30, 2012, http://dictionary.reference.com/browse/pastor?s=t.
171. 1 Corinthians 12:7 (NIV).
172. See Romans 12:3 (English Standard Version).
173. See 1 Peter 2:24–25 and note that the context is the removal of sin, the primary barrier to healing.
174. See 2 Corinthians 11:14.

246

175. See 1 Corinthians 14:4, 5, and 14.

176. See Romans 13:1 (NLT).

177. A. E. Weed, At the Foot of the Flatiron (American Mutoscope and Biograph Co., 1903), 35 mm film, from Library of Congress, The Life of a City: Early Films of New York, 1898–1906, MPEG video, 2:19, http://lcweb2. loc.gov/ammem/papr/nychome.html.]

178. See Romans 13:1 in the NLT.

179. George Barna's book *Revolution* is a perfect example of rebellion being made to sound spiritual. The entire book speaks of a new "breed" of Christ follower who's determined to "be" the church rather than be submitted to the primary representation of the church today. The concept of living out Christianity is good, but he continually glosses over the clear teaching of the New Testament and lauds resistance to authority, as well as accountability.

180. See Luke 23:34.

181. See Matthew 28:18–20.

182. See John 1:1 and 14.

183. See John 3:1–8.

184. See Matthew 28:18–20 and Mark 16:15–16 (emphasis added).

185. Case in point—Nicodemus in the third chapter of John's gospel.

186. See Ephesians 2:20 (NLT).

187. Acts 6:1–7.

188. Elders are referred to more than thirty times from Acts 14:23 to Jude. Elders' qualifications are found in 11 Timothy 3:1–7 and Titus 1:6–9; the qualifications for deacons are in 1 Timothy 3:8–13.

189. See Ephesians 4:11–12.

190. Ibid. plus verse 15 (NLT)

191. See Matthew 28:19–20.

192. See Acts 2:42–47 (NLT).

193. See Hebrews 13:17.
194. For a brief history of this movement, check "Self-Realization Fellowship," *Wikipedia*, accessed February 10, 2014, http://en.wikipedia.org/wiki/Self-Realization_Fellowship.
195. If you're unfamiliar with this movement, see http://www.has.vcu.edu/wrs/profiles/TranscendentalMeditation.htm for some explanation.
196. This is the fourth book of the Old Testament.
197. See Leviticus 9:24.
198. See *Bible Study Tools,* s.v. "zuwr," accessed February 12, 2014, http://www.biblestudytools.com/lexicons/hebrew/kjv/zuwr.html.
199. See Romans 6:23.
200. Quote is from the English Standard Version.
201. See 1 John 3:12 (NLT).
202. See Hebrews 11:4.
203. Jack Hayford, *The Reward of Worship: The Joy of Fellowship with a Personal God,* (Ada, Michigan: Chosen Books, 2007), 202.
204. See Romans 6:23 (NLT) and note the singular word, *sin,* not *sins.*
205. See Mathew 5:48.

The Challenge

206. See 1 Timothy 3:15. Note that's *the* truth, not my truth, your truth, or even a truth.
207. See Ephesians 3:10.
208. See Ephesians 2:8–9 (NLT).
209. See James 2:19 (NLT).
210. See John 3:16 in the Amplified Version.
211. Watchman Nee, *A Balanced Christian Life,* (New York: Christian Fellowship Publishers, Inc., 1981), 154.
212. Maurice Lednecky, *The DNA of Faith,* (Self-published, 2003), 59.

213. John Piper, *What Jesus Demands from the World* (Wheaton, Illinois: Crossway Books, 2006), 100–101.

214. Adrian Rogers, *How to Fortify Your Faith* (Memphis, Tennessee: Love Worth Finding Ministries, 2010), 3.

215. Ibid, 12.